Interactive Homework Workbook

Grade 3

Scott Foresman • Addison Wesley

enVisionMATH™

Scott Foresman
is an imprint of

pearsonschool.com

Editorial Offices: Glenview, Illinois • Parsippany, New Jersey • New York, New York
Sales Offices: Boston, Massachusetts • Duluth, Georgia • Glenview, Illinois
Coppell, Texas • Sacramento, California • Mesa, Arizona

ISBN – 13: 978-0-328-34176-4

ISBN – 10: 0-328-34176-2

9 10 V004 12 11

Contents

Name ______________________

Hundreds

Write each number in standard form.

1. ______

2. 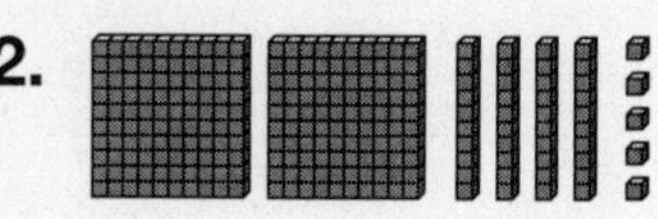 ______

3. 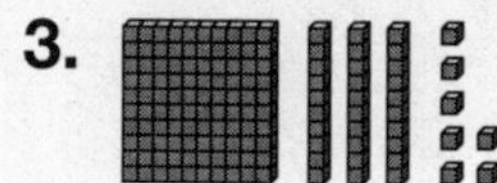 ______

4. 600 + 70 + 9 ______

5. 800 + 3 ______

6. four hundred thirty-one ______

Write each number in expanded form.

7. 392 ______

8. 710 ______

Write each number in word form.

9. 539 ______

10. 904 ______

11. **Algebra** Find the value of the missing number.

    462 = 400 + ☐ + 2

12. **Explain It** Why are five hundreds and three ones written as 503?

    ______

    ______

    ______

13. **Number Sense** Which is the standard form of six hundred forty?

    A 64 **B** 604 **C** 614 **D** 640

Name ______________________

Thousands

Write each number in standard form.

1. 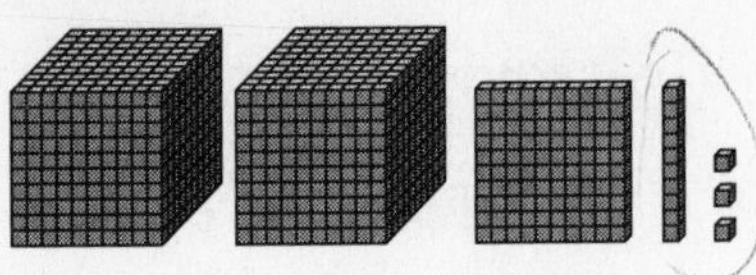

____

2. 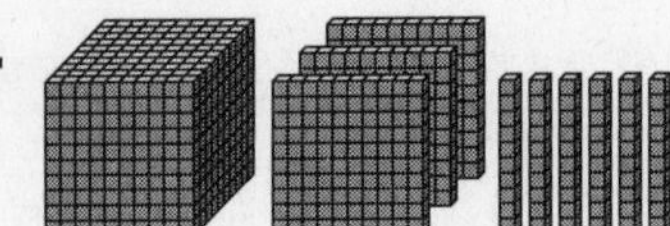

____

3. 3,000 + 900 + 40 + 7

____

4. 6,000 + 70 + 1

____

Write each number in expanded form.

5. 5,193

____

6. 4,308

____

Write the place of the underlined digit. Then write its value.

7. 5,$\underline{3}$42

____

8. $\underline{7}$,095

____

9. 6,3$\underline{9}$8

____

10. Explain It An arena can seat nine thousand, forty-eight people. How is that number written in standard form? Explain.

____

____

11. Number Sense Which is the word form of 8,040?

A eight hundred forty

B eight thousand, forty

C eight thousand, four

D eight thousand, four hundred

Name ______________________

Practice
1-3

Greater Numbers

Write each number in standard form.

1. seventy-five thousand, three hundred twelve ________

2. one hundred fourteen thousand, seven ________

3. 100,000 + 40,000 + 2,000 + 500 + 30 + 2 ________

4. 600,000 + 70,000 + 8,000 + 30 + 9 ________

Write each number in expanded form.

5. 73,581 ______________________

6. 390,062 ______________________

Write the place of the underlined digit. Then write its value.

7. 6<u>3</u>,219 ________ **8.** 3<u>8</u>2,407 ________ **9.** <u>9</u>72,362 ________

10. **Algebra** Find the missing number.

57,026 = 50,000 + ■ + 20 + 6 ________

11. **Explain It** Which is greater, the greatest whole number with 5 digits or the least whole number with 6 digits?

____

____

____

12. **Number Sense** Which is the word form for 280,309?

A two hundred eight thousand, three hundred ninety

B two hundred eighty thousand, thirty-nine

C two hundred eighty thousand, three hundred nine

D two hundred eighty thousand, three hundred ninety

Name ______________________

Practice 1-4

Ways to Name Numbers

Write the ordinal number and the ordinal word form of that number.

1. 26 ______________________
____

2. 43 ______________________
____

3. 51 ______________________
____

4. 60 ______________________
____

Name the number in two ways.

5. 3,600 ______________________
____
____

6. 4,700 ______________________
____
____

7. 6,900 ______________________
____
____

8. 9,400 ______________________
____
____

9. **Number Sense** The population of St. Louis, MO, is 344,362 and the population of Newark, NJ, is 280,666. Which city has the greater population?

____

10. The Coopers live at one thousand, seven hundred six South Central Avenue. How do you write the number of the Cooper's home?

____

11. Albert is running in a race. There are 21 people ahead of him. Write the ordinal number and the ordinal word form for Albert's place in line.

____

12. What is another way to write 7,600?

A seven thousand, six

B seventy-six hundred

C seven thousand, sixty

D seventy-six thousand

Name ______________________________

Practice **1-5**

Comparing Numbers

Compare the numbers. Use <, >, or =.

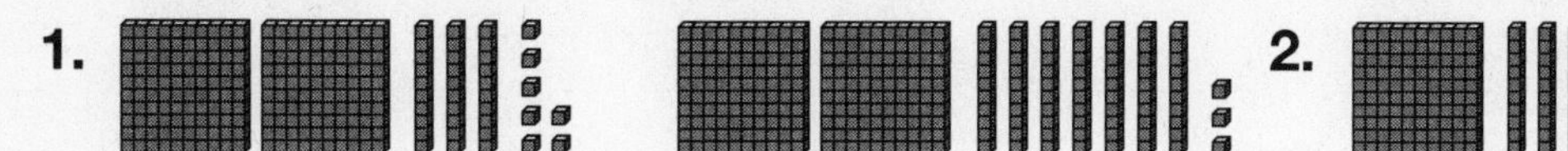

1. 237 _____ 273

2. 130 _____ 113

3. 725 ◯ 739 **4.** 831 ◯ 813 **5.** 926 ◯ 926

6. 2,734 ◯ 2,347 **7.** 4,827 ◯ 583 **8.** 5,327 ◯ 5,372

Use the table for **9** and **10**.

9. Between which pair of cities is the distance the greatest? See table.

____

____

Distance in Miles

New York, NY, to Rapid City, SD	1,701
Rapid City, SD, to Miami, FL	2,167
Miami, FL, to Seattle, WA	3,334
Portland, OR, to Little Rock, AR	2,217

10. Explain It Which has a greater distance, Rapid City to Miami or Portland to Little Rock? Which digits did you use to compare? See table.

____

____

Number Sense Write the missing digits to make each number sentence true.

11. 7☐7 < 713 **12.** 8☐5 > 889 **13.** 3,☐64 = 3,2☐4

14. Which sentence is true?

A 4,375 > 4,722 **C** 5,106 = 5,160

B 6,372 > 6,327 **D** 7,095 < 795

15. Which number is greater than 8,264?

A 8,246 **B** 8,275 **C** 6,842 **D** 8,195

Name ______________________

Practice 1-6

Ordering Numbers

Order the numbers from least to greatest.

1. 216 208 222

______

2. 3,795 3,659 3,747

______

Order the numbers from greatest to least.

3. 633 336 363

______

4. 5,017 5,352 5,193

______

Use the table for **5** through **7**.

5. Number Sense New Hampshire has a land area of 8,968 square miles. Which states in the table have a greater land area than New Hampshire?

______

______

Land Areas (in square miles)

State	Land Area
Maryland	9,774
Massachusetts	7,840
New Jersey	7,417
Vermont	9,250

6. Order the states in the table from greatest to least land area.

______

7. Explain It The Amazon River is 4,000 miles long. The Yangtze River is 3,964 miles long and the Nile River is 4,145 miles long. Write the steps you would use to order the lengths of the rivers from greatest to least.

______

______

8. Which number is between 6,532 and 6,600?

A 6,570 **B** 6,523 **C** 6,325 **D** 5,623

9. Which number makes this sentence true?
4,735 < ______ < 4,820

A 4,396 **B** 4,758 **C** 4,832 **D** 4,915

Name ____________________

Practice
1-7

Counting Money

Write the total value in dollars and cents.

1.    ________

2. 1 one-dollar bill, 2 quarters, 2 dimes, 1 nickel, 3 pennies

____

3. 2 one-dollar bills, 3 quarters, 2 dimes, 2 pennies

____

4. 1 five-dollar bill, one half dollar, 3 quarters, 1 nickel

____

5. 1 five-dollar bill, 2 one-dollar bills, 3 dimes, 3 nickels

____

Compare the amounts. Write <, >, or =.

6. $1.55 ◯ 1 one-dollar bill, 2 quarters

7. $1.90 ◯ 8 quarters

8. **Reasoning** Claire has 5 coins worth $0.61. What coins does she have?

____

9. Mark has 6 bills worth $14.00. What bills does he have?

____

10. What is the least number of coins you can use to show $0.37?

____

11. Which is equal to exactly $1.00?

A 3 quarters and 2 dimes

B 2 quarters, 2 dimes, and 2 nickels

C 1 half dollar, 1 quarter, and 1 dime

D 1 half dollar and 5 dimes

12. **Explain It** How can $0.60 be shown two different ways using only 3 coins each time?

____

Name ____________________

Practice
1-8

Making Change

List the coins and bills to make the change. Write the amount of change.

1. Cost: $0.64
Amount paid: $1.00

____

____

2. Cost: $1.18
Amount paid: $2.00

____

____

3. Cost: $2.89
Amount paid: $5.00

____

____

4. Cost: $4.04
Amount paid: $5.00

____

____

5. **Algebra** Alice paid for a newspaper with a $1 bill. She received $0.35 in change. How much money did the newspaper cost?

____

6. **Reasonableness** A new hair clip costs $1.60. Janice paid with 2 one-dollar bills. She received 3 coins back in change. What were they?

____

7. **Explain It** If pencils cost $0.26 each, could you buy four pencils with $1.00? Explain.

____

____

8. Lizzie is going to buy a ruler for $0.55 with a one-dollar bill. Marcy said Lizzie should get 1 quarter and 2 dimes for change. Patti said Lizzie should get 4 dimes and a nickel for change. Who is correct: Marcy, Patti, both, or neither?

____

9. Johnny bought a magazine for $3.24. He paid with a $5 bill. Which should be his change?

A $1.76 **C** $2.76
B $1.86 **D** $2.86

Name ______________________

Problem Solving: Make an Organized List

Make an organized list to solve.

1. List all the 3-digit numbers that fit these clues.
   - The hundreds digit is less than 3.
   - The tens digit is less than 2.
   - The ones digit is greater than 7.

   ____

   ____

2. List all the 4-digit numbers that fit these clues.
   - The thousands digit is greater than 8.
   - The hundreds digit is less than 4.
   - The tens and ones digits are the same as the thousands digit.

   ____

   ____

3. Jim and Sarah are running for class president. Cayla and Daniel are running for vice president. What combinations of president and vice president could there be?

   ____

   ____

   ____

4. List the ways that you can arrange the letters A, B, and C.

   ____

   ____

5. **Reasoning** What is this 3-digit number?
   - The hundreds digit is 4 greater than 3.
   - The tens digit is 1 more than the hundreds digit.
   - The ones digit is 3 less than the tens digit.

   ____

6. In how many ways can you make 30 cents using quarters, dimes, or nickels?

   A 4

   B 5

   C 6

   D 8

Name ______________________

Practice
2-1

Addition Meaning and Properties

Write each missing number.

1. 7 + 2 = 2 + ■ ______

2. 3 + ■ = 3 ______

3. (2 + 4) + 5 = 2 + (■ + 5) ______

4. 3 + ■ = 5 + 3 ______

5. ■ + 0 = 6 ______

6. (5 + 3) + 9 = 8 + ■ ______

7. **Reasoning** What property of addition is shown in the following number sentence? Explain.

7 + (3 + 5) = (7 + 3) + 5

____

____

8. **Number Sense** Minnie has 6 country CDs and 5 rock CDs. Amanda has 5 rock CDs and 6 country CDs. Who has more CDs? Explain.

____

____

9. Show how the Commutative Property of Addition works using the numbers 2, 3, and 5.

____

10. **Explain It** Jake says that adding 0 does not change a sum. Is he correct? Explain.

____

____

11. Which property of addition is shown by 5 + 2 = 2 + 5?

A Associative Property
B Distributive Property
C Commutative Property
D Identity Property

Name ______________________

Practice 2-2

Adding on a Hundred Chart

Use a hundred chart to add.

1	2	3	4	5	6	7	8	9	10
11	12	13	14	15	16	17	18	19	20
21	22	23	24	25	26	27	28	29	30
31	32	33	34	35	36	37	38	39	40
41	42	43	44	45	46	47	48	49	50
51	52	53	54	55	56	57	58	59	60
61	62	63	64	65	66	67	68	69	70
71	72	73	74	75	76	77	78	79	80
81	82	83	84	85	86	87	88	89	90
91	92	93	94	95	96	97	98	99	100

1. 45 + 30 ______

2. 36 + 33 ______

3. 52 + 46 ______

4. 27 + 23 ______

5. 36 + 45 ______

6. 49 + 24 ______

Number Sense Compare. Use <, >, or =.

7. 32 + 40 ◯ 42 + 38

8. 27 + 52 ◯ 52 + 27

9. 46 + 34 ◯ 33 + 45

10. 22 + 54 ◯ 28 + 48

11. 37 + 44 ◯ 32 + 50

12. 51 + 25 ◯ 41 + 25

13. **Number Sense** Mickey lives 35 miles away from his grandparents' home. His Aunt Roz lives 24 miles farther than his grandparents. How far does Mickey live from his Aunt Roz?

____

14. Kirsten spent 45 minutes doing her math homework and 35 minutes studying for science class. How much time did Kirsten spend studying all together? ______________

15. Which addition problem has a sum of 65?

A 37 + 28 **B** 46 + 29 **C** 34 + 32 **D** 27 + 39

Name ______________________________

Using Mental Math to Add

Use breaking apart to add mentally.

1. 53 + 34

34 = 30 + ☐

53 + ☐ = 83

83 + ☐ = 87

So, 53 + 34 = ☐

2. 42 + 29

29 = 20 + ☐

42 + ☐ = 62

☐ + 9 = 71

So, 42 + 29 = ☐

3. 47 + 41

41 = ☐ + 1

47 + ☐ = 87

☐ + 1 = 88

So, 47 + 41 = ☐

Make a ten to add mentally.

4. 27 + 24

24 = 3 + ☐

27 + ☐ = 30

☐ + 21 = 51

So, 27 + 24 = ☐

5. 54 + 19

19 = ☐ + 6

☐ + 6 = 60

60 + ☐ = 73

So, 54 + 19 = ☐

6. 38 + 27

27 = ☐ + 25

38 + ☐ = 40

40 + ☐ = 65

So, 38 + 27 = ☐

Find each sum using mental math.

7. 52 + 26 ______

8. 47 + 8 ______

9. 32 + 17 ______

10. 28 + 31 ______

11. 43 + 38 ______

12. 72 + 7 ______

13. 42 + 33 ______

14. 36 + 14 ______

15. **Number Sense** Ashton broke apart a number into 30 + 7. What number did he start with? ______

16. What is the sum of 27 + 42 using mental math?

A 68 **B** 69 **C** 78 **D** 79

Name ______________________

Practice
2-4

Rounding

Round to the nearest ten.

1. 37 ______ **2.** 93 ______ **3.** 78 ______ **4.** 82 ______ **5.** 24 ______

6. 426 ______ **7.** 329 ______ **8.** 815 ______ **9.** 163 ______ **10.** 896 ______

Round to the nearest hundred.

11. 395 ______ **12.** 638 ______ **13.** 782 ______ **14.** 246 ______ **15.** 453 ______

16. 529 ______ **17.** 877 ______ **18.** 634 ______ **19.** 329 ______ **20.** 587 ______

21. **Number Sense** Tyrell says 753 rounds to 800. Sara says 753 rounds to 750. Who is correct? Explain.

____

____

22. **Explain It** How would you use a number line to round 148 to the nearest ten.

____

____

23. There are 254 counties in Texas. What is that number rounded to the nearest ten? What is that number rounded to the nearest hundred?

____

24. Which number does not round to 400?

A 347 **B** 369 **C** 413 **D** 448

Name ________________________

Practice 2-5

Estimating Sums

Round to the nearest ten to estimate.

1. 58 + 43 ______ **2.** 87 + 69 ______ **3.** 37 + 141 ______ **4.** 422 + 296 ______

Round to the nearest hundred to estimate.

5. 536 + 393 ______ **6.** 242 + 359 ______ **7.** 713 + 82 ______ **8.** 313 + 405 ______

Use compatible numbers to estimate. Sample answers are given. Accept reasonable answers.

9. 83 + 34 ______ **10.** 329 + 64 ______ **11.** 212 + 347 ______ **12.** 537 + 244 ______

13. Reasonableness Miguel has 325 baseball cards and 272 football cards. He said that he has 597 cards in all. Is his answer reasonable? Explain using estimation.

____

____

____

14. Write a Problem Natalie has 138 DVDs and 419 CDs. If you were to estimate the sum of the DVDs and CDs, what sentence could you write? Then find your estimated sum.

____

15. Which of the following shows estimating 287 + 491 by using compatible numbers?

A 100 + 500 **B** 300 + 400 **C** 280 + 400 **D** 280 + 500

Name ____________________

Practice

2-8

Adding 3-Digit Numbers

Estimate. Then find each sum.

1. 329 + 468

2. 148 + 231

3. 555 + 222

4. 472 + 515

5. 396 + 428

6. 645 + 79

7. 536 + 399

8. 268 + 422

9. 633 + 210

10. **Critical Thinking** Follow the steps below to find how many combined points were scored by Howie and Theo.

a. Write a number sentence to show how to solve the problem.

____

b. Estimate the total points scored by Howie and Theo.

____

c. Find the actual total. ____________________

11. **Explain It** Write an addition story for two 3-digit numbers. Write the answer to your story.

____

12. Sharon can run 278 yards in one minute. Pete can run 145 more yards than Sharon in one minute. How many yards can Pete run in one minute?

____

13. There were 752 people at a town meeting last week. There were 163 more people this week. How many people attended this week's meeting?

A 815 **B** 825 **C** 915 **D** 925

Name ______________________

Practice 2-9

Adding 3 or More Numbers

Find each sum.

1. 75 + 36 + 58

2. 142 + 297 + 116

3. 524 + 97 + 176

4. 273 + 187 + 64 + 249

5. 319 + 48 + 136 + 347

6. 237 + 75 + 49 ______

7. 49 + 7 + 63 + 8 ______

8. 143 + 47 + 219 + 136 ______

9. Estimation Estimate the sum of 327 + 419 + 173.

____

10. Number Sense Justine has 162 red buttons, 98 blue buttons, and 284 green buttons. She says she knows she has more than 500 buttons without adding. Do you agree? Explain.

____

____

11. Carlos ate or drank everything that is listed in the table. How many calories did Carlos consume?

______

Food	Amount	Calories
Bran flakes	1 ounce	90
Banana	1	105
Orange juice	1 cup	110
Milk	1 cup	150

12. In winning the 1884 U.S. presidential election, Grover Cleveland received 219 electoral votes. He received 168 electoral votes in 1888, and lost. Then he received 277 electoral votes and won in 1892. How many electoral votes did Cleveland receive in all?

______

13. Kyle has 378 pennies, 192 nickels, and 117 dimes. How many coins does he have all together?

A 495 **B** 570 **C** 677 **D** 687

Name ___________________________

Practice
2-10

Problem Solving: Draw a Picture

1. Kelly bought a CD for $15 and a book for $13. How much money did Kelly spend in all?

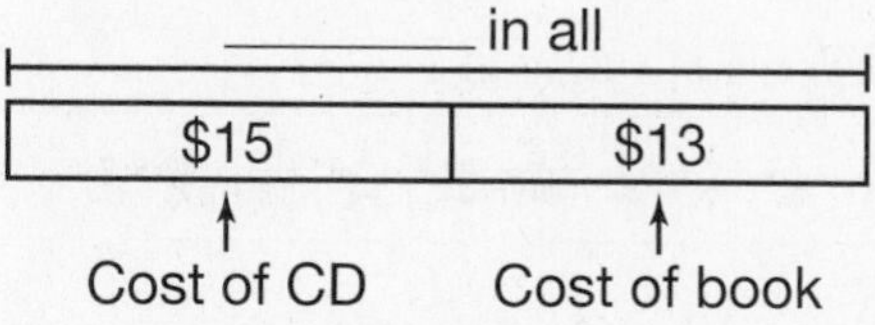

2. **Estimation** There are 28 students in the chorus and 31 students in the band. All will be performing tonight. About how many students will be performing in all?

_______ students in all

30	30

Chorus Band

3. Jane sold 25 raffle tickets Monday, 30 raffle tickets Tuesday, and 40 raffle tickets Wednesday. How many raffle tickets did Jane sell all together?

_______ tickets in all

25	30	40

4. Dan cycled 12 miles Saturday and 18 miles Sunday. How many miles did he cycle all together?

_______ miles in all

12	18

5. How many students belong to the Spanish and Science clubs?

_______ members in all

Club Membership

Club	Members
Math	24
Spanish	18
Running	15
Science	6

6. About how many students belong to the Math and Spanish clubs?

_______ members in all

7. How many students belong to the Math, Running, and Science clubs?

_______ members in all

Name ____________________

Practice
3-1

Subtraction Meanings

Write a number sentence for each situation. Solve.

1. Terrance has 14 CDs. Robyn has 9 CDs. How many more CDs does Terrance have than Robyn?

◎◎◎◎◎◎◎◎◎	?
◎◎◎◎◎◎◎◎◎◎◎◎◎◎	

____

2. How many more black stars are there than white stars?

☆☆☆☆☆☆☆	?
★★★★★★★★★★★	

____

3. Arizona has 15 counties. Connecticut has 8 counties. How many more counties does Arizona have than Connecticut?

____

4. A baseball hat costs $12. Nancy has a coupon for $4 off. How much money will Nancy spend on the baseball hat?

____

5. **Draw a Picture** Carrie invited 13 girls to a party. Five of the girls have already arrived. How many girls have yet to arrive? Draw a picture to show the problem.

____

6. **Number Sense** Write the fact family for 3, 9, and 12.

____

____

____

____

7. LaToya has 12 postcards and 4 photographs on a bulletin board. How many more postcards does LaToya have than photographs?

A 7 **B** 8 **C** 9 **D** 16

Name ____________________

Practice 3-2

Subtracting on a Hundred Chart

Use a hundred chart to subtract.

1	2	3	4	5	6	7	8	9	10
11	12	13	14	15	16	17	18	19	20
21	22	23	24	25	26	27	28	29	30
31	32	33	34	35	36	37	38	39	40
41	42	43	44	45	46	47	48	49	50
51	52	53	54	55	56	57	58	59	60
61	62	63	64	65	66	67	68	69	70
71	72	73	74	75	76	77	78	79	80
81	82	83	84	85	86	87	88	89	90
91	92	93	94	95	96	97	98	99	100

1. 53 − 20 ______

2. 76 − 40 ______

3. 73 − 30 ______

4. 67 − 50 ______

5. 94 − 26 ______

6. 34 − 18 ______

7. 56 − 24 ______

8. 84 − 39 ______

9. 63 − 49 ______

10. 77 − 40 ______

11. 93 − 55 ______

12. 64 − 36 ______

13. At full speed, a lion can run 50 miles per hour. A grizzly bear can run 30 miles per hour. How much faster can a lion run than a grizzly bear? ______ miles per hour

14. **Reasonableness** Bobby subtracted 75 − 45 and said the difference is 30. Is his answer reasonable? Why or why not?

____

____

15. By how many points did the Terriers win?

______

16. Which subtraction sentence has a difference of 34?

A 57 − 33 = ■

B 61 − 17 = ■

C 72 − 37 ■

D 63 − 29 = ■

Name ____________________

Practice
3-3

Using Mental Math to Subtract

Find each difference using mental math.

1. 38 − 14 ______ **2.** 42 − 13 ______ **3.** 55 − 12 ______ **4.** 62 − 17 ______

5. 72 − 19 ______ **6.** 94 − 11 ______ **7.** 32 − 15 ______ **8.** 85 − 18 ______

9. 43 − 16 ______ **10.** 66 − 15 ______ **11.** 53 − 19 ______ **12.** 72 − 16 ______

13. **Number Sense** Gillian started solving 88 − 29. This is what she did.

$88 - 29 = ?$
$88 - 30 = 58$

What should Gillian do next? ____________________

14. **Explain It** Tell how to find 81 − 16 using mental math.

____

____

____

15. Tiffany will use a total of 63 tiles for her art project. She only needs 17 more tiles. Use mental math to find how many tiles she has already.

____

16. To solve 35 − 19, Jack used 35 − 20 and then

A added 1.

B subtracted 9.

C subtracted 1.

D added 9.

Name ______________________

Practice
3-4

Estimating Differences

Round to the nearest hundred to estimate each difference.

1. 478 − 267 ______

2. 236 − 119 ______

3. 588 − 321 ______

Round to the nearest ten to estimate each difference.

4. 677 − 421 ______

5. 296 − 97 ______

6. 312 − 157 ______

Use compatible numbers to estimate each difference.

7. 84 − 36 ______

8. 427 − 163 ______

9. 609 − 243 ______

10. **Number Sense** Fern rounded to the nearest ten to estimate 548 − 132. She subtracted 540 − 130 and got 410. Is Fern's estimate correct? Explain.

____

____

11. Waco, TX, has an elevation of 405 feet. Dallas, TX, has an elevation of 463 feet. About how many feet greater is Dallas's elevation than Waco's elevation? ______________

12. On Friday, 537 people attended a play. For Saturday's matinee, there were 812 people. About how many more people attended the play on Saturday than on Friday? ______________

13. A football team scored 529 points one season and then 376 points the next. About how many points less did the team score in the second season? Round to the nearest ten. ______

14. George got a 94 on his spelling test and a 68 on his math test. Which number sentence best shows about how many more points George got on his spelling test than on his math test?

A 90 − 60 = 30

B 90 + 70 = 160

C 100 + 60 = 160

D 90 − 70 = 20

Name ____________________

Practice 3-5

Problem Solving: Reasonableness

Solve. Then check that your answer is reasonable.

1. The Aggies scored 59 points in the first half and 56 points in the second half. How many points did the Aggies score altogether?

_______ points in all

59	56

2. Ms. Rice is driving 92 miles to a meeting. After driving 54 miles, she stops to buy gasoline. How many more miles does she have left?

92 miles in all

54	

3. There are 45 students going on a field trip. Of those students, 27 are from Mrs. Unser's class. The rest are from Mr. King's class. How many students are from Mr. King's class?

45 students in all

27	

4. **Estimation** In the 2004 Summer Olympics, the United States won 36 gold, 39 silver, and 27 bronze medals. About how many medals did the United States win?

_______ medals in all

40	40	30

5. Christine is reading a short story that is 76 pages long. She just finished reading page 47. How many more pages does she have left to read?

76 pages in all

47	

6. Wyoming has 23 counties. Wisconsin has 49 more counties than Wyoming. How many counties does Wisconsin have?

A 26 **B** 62 **C** 72 **D** 82

Name ____________________

Practice **4-1**

Models for Subtracting 2-Digit Numbers

Use the place-value blocks to subtract.

1. $\begin{array}{r} 54 \\ -\ 28 \\ \hline \end{array}$

2. 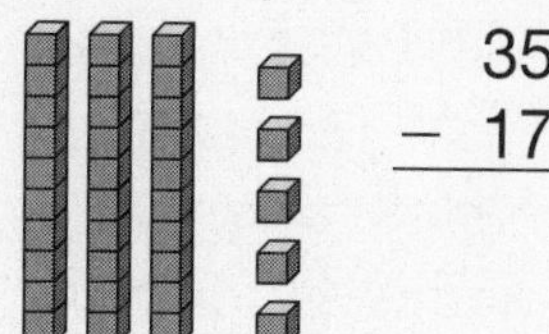 $\begin{array}{r} 35 \\ -\ 17 \\ \hline \end{array}$

Use place-value blocks or draw pictures to subtract.

3. $\begin{array}{r} 31 \\ -\ 12 \\ \hline \end{array}$ **4.** $\begin{array}{r} 56 \\ -\ 39 \\ \hline \end{array}$ **5.** $\begin{array}{r} 63 \\ -\ 42 \\ \hline \end{array}$ **6.** $\begin{array}{r} 37 \\ -\ 19 \\ \hline \end{array}$ **7.** $\begin{array}{r} 60 \\ -\ 32 \\ \hline \end{array}$

8. $\begin{array}{r} 44 \\ -\ 35 \\ \hline \end{array}$ **9.** $\begin{array}{r} 73 \\ -\ 47 \\ \hline \end{array}$ **10.** $\begin{array}{r} 55 \\ -\ 27 \\ \hline \end{array}$ **11.** $\begin{array}{r} 58 \\ -\ 23 \\ \hline \end{array}$ **12.** $\begin{array}{r} 61 \\ -\ 14 \\ \hline \end{array}$

13. Draw a Picture Draw two ways to show 43 using place-value blocks.

____

14. Melissa finished page 72 of her book today. She started at page 26. How many pages did she read today? __________

15. Pedro lives 67 miles from his grandparents. After 49 miles of driving, his family stopped for gas. How many miles does Pedro's family have left to reach his grandparents' home? __________

16. There were 45 students on a bus. At the first stop, 11 students got off. Another 17 students got off at the second stop. How many students are still on the bus?

A 7 **B** 17 **C** 28 **D** 34

Name ______________________________

Practice
4-2

Subtracting 2-Digit Numbers

Subtract.

1. $\begin{array}{r} 34 \\ -\ 16 \\ \hline \end{array}$ **2.** $\begin{array}{r} 43 \\ -\ 27 \\ \hline \end{array}$ **3.** $\begin{array}{r} 76 \\ -\ 28 \\ \hline \end{array}$ **4.** $\begin{array}{r} 65 \\ -\ 38 \\ \hline \end{array}$ **5.** $\begin{array}{r} 82 \\ -\ 47 \\ \hline \end{array}$

6. 82 − 67 = ________ **7.** 63 − 35 = ________ **8.** 86 − 42 = ________

9. Reasonableness Rebecca subtracted 47 − 28 and got 19. Is her answer reasonable? Explain.

____

____

____

10. Explain It Do you need to regroup to find 73 − 35? Explain your answer.

____

____

____

11. Write a Problem Bethany has 43 apples. Write a subtraction story about the apples that would require regrouping. Then write the answer in a complete sentence.

____

____

____

12. The tree farm had 65 shade trees for sale. It sold 39 of the trees. How many shade trees did the farm have left?

A 26 **B** 36 **C** 94 **D** 104

Name ______________________

Practice

4-5

Subtracting Across Zero

Find each difference.

1. 406 − 28

2. 300 − 211

3. 501 − 268

4. 705 − 347

5. 605 − 219

6. 800 − 579

7. 907 − 728

8. 603 − 347

9. 507 − 388

10. 706 − 497

11. 404 − 305 = ______ **12.** 501 − 223 = ______ **13.** 302 − 166 = ______

14. There were 600 ears of corn for sale at the produce market. At the end of the day, there were 212 ears left. How many ears of corn were sold? ______

15. Darrin has 702 CDs in his collection. Dana has 357 CDs in her collection. How many more CDs does Darrin have than Dana? ______

16. **Strategy Practice** Party Palace has an order for 505 party favors. It packaged 218 favors Saturday and 180 favors Sunday. How many more party favors does it still need to package? ______

17. **Write a Problem** Write a subtraction problem involving regrouping that has Ted reading 304 pages. Answer your question.

____

____

____

18. The Williams Tower in Houston, TX, is 901 feet tall. The Tower of the Americas in San Antonio, TX, is 622 feet tall. How much taller is the Williams Tower than the Tower of the Americas?

A 279 feet **B** 289 feet **C** 379 feet **D** 389 feet

Name ____________________

Practice

4-6

Problem Solving: Draw a Picture and Write a Number Sentence

The table below shows the areas of some of the smallest countries in the world. Use the table for **1–3.**

Area of Countries

Country	Area (in sq mi)
San Marino	24
Liechtenstein	62
Maldives	116
Palau	177

1. How many square miles greater is Maldives than San Marino?

116 square miles

24	______

2. Draw a Picture Draw a diagram to show how to find the difference between the areas of Liechtenstein and San Marino. Use your diagram to solve the problem.

3. Grenada is 15 square miles greater than Maldives. What is the area of Grenada?

______ square miles

116	15

4. There are 237 students at Johnson Elementary School. There are 188 students at Hoover Elementary School. How many more students are at Johnson than at Hoover?

237 students

188	______

5. Write a Problem Write a real-world problem that you can solve by adding or subtracting. Then give your problem to a classmate to solve.

____

____

____

Name ____________________

Practice 5-1

Multiplication as Repeated Addition

Complete.

1.

2 groups of ____

5 + ____ = ____

2 × ____ = ____

2.

3 groups of ____

4 + ____ + ____ = ____

3 × ____ = ____

3. 4 + 4 + 4 + 4 + 4 = 5 × ____

4. ____ + ____ + ____ = 3 × 8

5. 9 + ____ + ____ = ____ × 9

6. 7 + 7 + 7 + 7 = ____ × ____

Algebra Write +, −, or × for each ☐.

7. 5 ☐ 4 = 9

8. 6 ☐ 2 = 12

9. 7 ☐ 3 = 4

10. 3 ☐ 3 = 9

11. 8 ☐ 6 = 2

12. 3 ☐ 3 = 6

13. **Number Sense** Marlon has 4 cards, Jake has 4 cards, and Sam has 3 cards. Can you write a multiplication sentence to find how many cards they have in all? Explain.

____

____

14. **Write a Problem** Draw a picture that shows equal groups. Then write an addition sentence and a multiplication sentence for your picture.

15. Which is equal to 6 + 6 + 6 + 6?

A 6 × 3 **B** 3 × 6 **C** 4 × 6 **D** 6 × 5

Name ______________________

Practice 5-2

Arrays and Multiplication

Write a multiplication sentence for each array.

1. 

2. 

3. 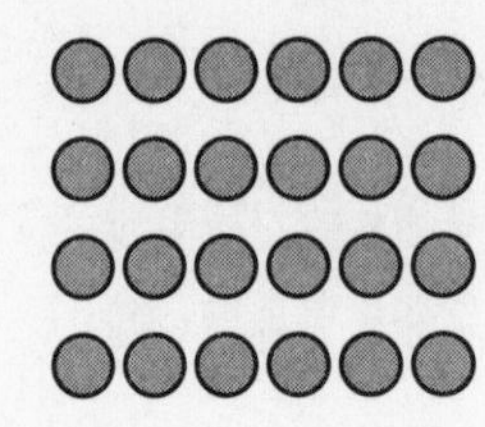

______________ ______________ ______________

Draw an array to find each multiplication fact. Write the product.

4. $3 \times 6 =$ ______

5. $4 \times 7 =$ ______

Complete each multiplication sentence.
Use counters or draw an array to help.

6. $3 \times$ ____ $= 21$

   $7 \times$ ____ $= 21$

7. $4 \times 9 =$ ____

   $9 \times 4 =$ ____

8. $5 \times 6 =$ ____

   $6 \times 5 =$ ____

9. $4 \times 7 =$ ____

   $7 \times 4 =$ ____

10. $6 \times 8 =$ ____

    $8 \times 6 =$ ____

11. $9 \times 5 =$ ____

    $5 \times 9 =$ ____

12. **Explain It** If you know that $7 \times 8 = 56$, how can you use the Commutative (Order) Property of Multiplication to find the product of 8×7?

____

____

____

____

13. Which of the following is equal to 8×4?

A 4×8 **B** $4 + 8$ **C** $8 - 4$ **D** $8 + 4$

Name ______________________

Using Multiplication to Compare

Find each amount. You may use drawings or counters to help.

1. 2 times as many as 5 ______

2. 3 times as many as 7 ______

3. 4 times as many as 6 ______

4. 3 times as many as 9 ______

5. twice as many as 8 ______

6. 5 times as many as 3 ______

7. 4 times as many as 7 ______

8. 5 times as many as 6 ______

9. 4 times as many as 3 ______

10. **Reasoning** John has 5 computer games. Julian has twice as many computer games as John. How many computer games do they have in all? ______

11. George Washington is on the $1 bill. Abraham Lincoln is on the bill that is worth 5 times as much as the $1 bill. What bill is Abraham Lincoln on? ______

12. Paula has twice as many guests this week as she did last week. Last week she had 7 guests. How many guests does she have this week? ______

13. John F. Kennedy is on the coin that is worth 5 times as much as a dime. What coin is John F. Kennedy on?

A nickel **B** quarter **C** half dollar **D** dollar

Name ______________________________

Writing Multiplication Stories

Write a multiplication story for each.

Draw a picture to find each product.

1. 3×6 **2.** 2×8 **3.** 4×3

Write a multiplication story for each picture.

4.

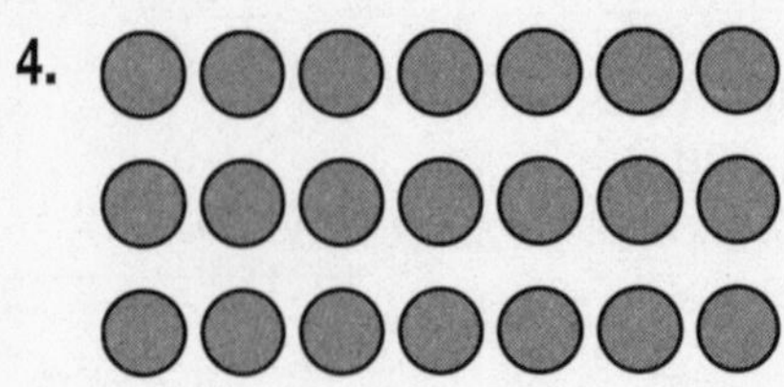

5.

6. Algebra Hot dog buns come in packages of 8. Mrs. Wilson has a total of 40 hot dog buns. Draw a picture to find how many packages of hot dog buns Mrs. Wilson has.

7. There are 9 players on a baseball team. At the park, 4 teams are playing. How many baseball players are playing at the park?

A 27 **B** 32 **C** 36 **D** 40

Name ______________________

Practice **5-5**

Problem Solving: Writing to Explain

1. Look at the numbers below.
13, 15, 19, 25, …

a. Describe the pattern.

____

____

____

b. Explain how you can find the next two numbers. What are the next two numbers?

____

____

2. Mr. Wilson is setting up volleyball teams. There are 6 players on a team.

a. Complete the table below.

Teams	1	2	3	4	5
Players	6	12	18		

b. Explain how the number of players changes as the number of teams changes.

____

____

____

3. Algebra The table below shows the amount of money that Louise earns in allowance each week.

a. Complete the table.

Louise's Allowance

Number of Weeks	Allowance
1	$8
2	$16
3	$24
4	
5	

b. How did the table help you to find the pattern?

____

____

4. Diana is training to run a marathon.

a. Complete the table for Diana's first week of training.

Diana's Training Schedule

Day	Minutes
Monday	15
Tuesday	20
Wednesday	25
Thursday	
Friday	

b. If she continues the pattern, for how many minutes will Diana run on Saturday?

____

Name ______________________________

Practice 5-6

2 and 5 as Factors

Find each product.

1. 2×5 ______ **2.** 4×5 ______ **3.** 3×2 ______ **4.** 8×5 ______ **5.** 7×2 ______

6. 9×2 **7.** 6×5 **8.** 5×9 **9.** 2×6 **10.** 5×5

11. Multiply 7 and 5. ______

12. Find 8 times 2. ______

Algebra Compare. Use <, >, or =.

13. 3×5 ◯ 4×5 **14.** 6×3 ◯ 6×2 **15.** 8×2 ◯ 2×8

16. 6×5 ◯ 5×6 **17.** 4×2 ◯ 5×2 **18.** 7×5 ◯ 5×6

19. Tara walks 2 miles each day. How many miles does she walk in a week?

______

20. There are 5 days in each school week. How many school days are there in 9 weeks?

______

21. Explain It How can adding doubles help you to multiply by 2? Give an example in your explanation.

____

____

____

____

22. If the ones digit of a number greater than 1 is 0, what factor or factors must that number have?

A 2 only **B** 5 only **C** 2 and 5 **D** Neither 2 or 5

Name ______________________

Practice 5-7

10 as a Factor

Find each product.

1. 3×10 ____ **2.** 7×10 ____ **3.** 10×5 ____ **4.** 7×5 ____ **5.** 10×8 ____

6. 9×10 ____ **7.** 6×1 ____ **8.** 10×2 ____ **9.** 9×7 ____ **10.** 4×10 ____

11. 1×10 ____ **12.** 6×10 ____ **13.** 5×4 ____ **14.** 10×10 ____ **15.** 10×3 ____

16. 8×5 **17.** 10×9 **18.** 10×8 **19.** 10×4 **20.** 10×7

21. 10×6 **22.** 5×2 **23.** 10×1 **24.** 10×5 **25.** 9×0

26. Mary Ann earns $10 each day walking the neighborhood dogs. How much will she earn in 7 days?

____

27. A game of basketball requires 10 players. At the park, there are 5 games being played. How many total players are at the park?

____

28. **Strategy Practice** Mr. Keyes made four rows of 10 cookies. Seven of the cookies in the first row were eaten. How many cookies remain?

____

29. Which is **NOT** a multiple of 10?

A 30

B 55

C 70

D 90

Name ______________________

Practice
5-8

9 as a Factor

Find each product.

1. 9×4 ______ **2.** 7×9 ______ **3.** 9×9 ______ **4.** 9×8 ______ **5.** 5×3 ______

6. $\begin{array}{r} 9 \\ \times 5 \\ \hline \end{array}$ **7.** $\begin{array}{r} 2 \\ \times 9 \\ \hline \end{array}$ **8.** $\begin{array}{r} 6 \\ \times 9 \\ \hline \end{array}$ **9.** $\begin{array}{r} 2 \\ \times 7 \\ \hline \end{array}$ **10.** $\begin{array}{r} 8 \\ \times 9 \\ \hline \end{array}$

11. Multiply 4 and 9. ______

12. Find 3 times 9. ______

Algebra Complete. Use +, −, or ×.

13. $2 \times 9 = 10 \square 8$

14. $20 + 16 = 9 \square 4$

15. $9 \times 5 = 50 \square 5$

16. $9 \times 8 = 70 \square 2$

17. $10 \square 1 = 1 \times 9$

18. $9 \square 3 = 20 + 7$

19. Paula's hair was put into 9 braids. Each braid used 3 beads. How many beads were used in all?

____

20. A baseball game has 9 innings. A doubleheader is 2 games in the same day. How many innings are there in a doubleheader?

____

21. Write a Problem Write a multiplication story for 9×8. Include the product in your story.

____

____

22. Which number below is a multiple of 9?

A 35 **B** 46 **C** 54 **D** 65

Name ______________________

Practice 5-9

Multiplying with 0 and 1

Find each product.

1. 1×4 ______ **2.** 0×5 ______ **3.** 6×1 ______ **4.** 0×3 ______ **5.** 5×1 ______

6. $\begin{array}{r} 1 \\ \times 1 \\ \hline \end{array}$ **7.** $\begin{array}{r} 0 \\ \times 9 \\ \hline \end{array}$ **8.** $\begin{array}{r} 1 \\ \times 8 \\ \hline \end{array}$ **9.** $\begin{array}{r} 6 \\ \times 1 \\ \hline \end{array}$ **10.** $\begin{array}{r} 7 \\ \times 0 \\ \hline \end{array}$

11. Multiply 1 and 7. ______

12. Find 0 times 8. ______

Algebra Complete. Write <, >, or = for each ◯.

13. 1×6 ◯ 3×0 **14.** 5×0 ◯ 1×7 **15.** 1×3 ◯ 3×1

Algebra Complete. Write ×, +, or − for each □.

16. 1 □ 7 = 7 **17.** 8 □ 0 = 8 **18.** 6 □ 1 = 5

19. Sara keeps 4 boxes under her bed. Each box is for holding a different type of seashell. There are 0 shells in each box. Write a multiplication sentence to show how many shells Sara has in all.

____

20. **Explain It** Is the product of 0×0 the same as the sum of $0 + 0$? Explain.

____

____

21. **Geometry** A pentagon has 5 sides. Lonnie has a table shaped like a pentagon. How many chairs does Lonnie need if he wants 1 chair on each side?

______

22. Which multiplication problem below has the greatest product?

A 5×1 **B** 6×0 **C** 0×7 **D** 8×0

Name ______________________

Practice
5-10

Problem Solving: Two-Question Problems

Use the answer from the first problem to solve the second problem.

1a. Lynette bought a book for $13 and a DVD for $22. How much money did the items cost?

_______ in all

$22	$13

1b. Suppose Lynette paid the cashier with a $50 bill. How much change should Lynette get?

$50 in all

$35	_______

2a. Melissa bought 2 T-shirts for $9 each. How much money did Melissa spend on T-shirts?

____

b. Melissa had $32 in her purse. How much money does she have left?

____

3a. Curt bought 3 tickets to the movies for $8 each. How much money did Curt spend on movie tickets?

____

b. Curt also bought a large popcorn for $5. How much money did Curt spend altogether?

____

4. Lenny bought 4 packs of baseball cards for $3 each. He paid the cashier with a $20 bill. How much change will Lenny receive?

A $7

B $8

C $12

D $13

5. **Write a Problem** Write two problems that can be solved by using the answer from the first problem to solve the second problem.

____

____

____

____

____

Name ______________________

3 as a Factor

Find the product.

1. 1×3 ______
2. 3×7 ______
3. 6×3 ______
4. 8×3 ______
5. 10×5 ______
6. 3×2 ______
7. 4×3 ______
8. 3×0 ______
9. 2×7 ______
10. 3×3 ______
11. 5×3
12. 10×3
13. 2×3
14. 3×9
15. 9×3

16. A bicycle store also sells tricycles. It has 6 tricycles in stock. How many wheels do the tricycles have in all? ______

17. There were 5 people who bought tickets to a football game. They bought 3 tickets each. How many tickets were bought altogether? ______

18. **Number Sense** What addition sentence is equal to 4×3? ______

19. **Geometry** How many small squares are in the figure below?

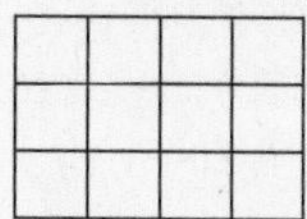

20. **Reasonableness** Maria said $7 \times 3 = 21$. Connie said $3 \times 7 = 21$. Who is correct? Explain.

______

______

______

21. Which number is a multiple of 3?

A 16 **B** 20 **C** 24 **D** 28

Name ____________________

Practice **6-2**

4 as a Factor

Find the product.

1. 2×4 ______ **2.** 4×5 ______ **3.** 3×4 ______ **4.** 4×4 ______ **5.** 5×8 ______

6. 4×6 ______ **7.** 1×4 ______ **8.** 3×9 ______ **9.** 0×4 ______ **10.** 4×7 ______

11. $\begin{array}{r} 10 \\ \times\ 4 \\ \hline \end{array}$ **12.** $\begin{array}{r} 1 \\ \times\ 4 \\ \hline \end{array}$ **13.** $\begin{array}{r} 2 \\ \times\ 4 \\ \hline \end{array}$ **14.** $\begin{array}{r} 4 \\ \times\ 9 \\ \hline \end{array}$ **15.** $\begin{array}{r} 8 \\ \times\ 4 \\ \hline \end{array}$

16. Number Sense What multiplication fact can you double to find 4×7?

______

17. Each square table can seat 4 people. How many people can be seated at 8 square tables?

______

18. Jillian sold 4 books of raffle tickets. Each book had 9 tickets. How many tickets did Jillian sell all together?

______

19. The soccer team has practice 4 times each week during the season. If the season is 10 weeks long, how many practices does the team have?

______

20. Writing to Explain If you know that $4 \times 5 = 20$, how can you use the Commutative (Order) Property to find 5×4?

______

______

______

21. Aaron changed the tires on 5 cars. Each car had 4 tires. How many tires did Aaron change?

A 12 **B** 16 **C** 20 **D** 24

Name ______________________

Practice

6-3

6 and 7 as Factors

Find the product.

1. 5×6 ______
2. 6×3 ______
3. 6×8 ______
4. 3×7 ______
5. 7×10 ______
6. 7×4 ______
7. 6×4 ______
8. 5×7 ______
9. 7×8 ______
10. 6×6 ______
11. 7×6
12. 10×6
13. 10×7
14. 7×7
15. 2×6

16. **Number Sense** What multiplication fact can be found by using the arrays for 2×9 and 5×9?

______

17. The chicken eggs Raul's science class is watching take 3 weeks to hatch. How many days will it be until the eggs hatch?

______

18. Emily cut 7 apples into slices. There are 6 slices from each apple. How many apple slices does she have in all?

______

19. At a barbeque there are 6 tables set up. Each table can seat 8 people. How many people can be seated at the tables all together?

______

20. **Writing to Explain** How could you use $5 \times 6 = 30$ to find the product of 6×6?

____

____

____

21. Barry takes 7 minutes to ride his bicycle one mile. At this rate, how long would Barry take to ride his bicycle 4 miles?

A 21 minutes **B** 24 minutes **C** 27 minutes **D** 28 minutes

Name ______________________

Practice 6-4

8 as a Factor

Find the product.

1. 1×8 ______
2. 8×0 ______
3. 4×6 ______
4. 2×8 ______
5. 8×7 ______
6. 8×3 ______
7. 4×8 ______
8. 8×9 ______
9. 8×5 ______
10. 8×8 ______
11. 10×8
12. 7×8
13. 7×6
14. 8×3
15. 9×8

16. An octopus has 8 arms. At the zoo, there are 3 octopuses in one tank. How many arms do the octopuses have all together? ______

17. **Number Sense** How can you use 4×7 to find 8×7? Find the product.

____

____

18. **Writing to Explain** Jose said all of the multiples of 8 are also multiples of 2. Jamila said that all of the multiples of 8 are also multiples of 4. Who is correct? Explain.

____

____

19. A package of fruit juice contains 8 boxes. How many boxes are there in 5 packages? ______

20. What is the next number in the pattern below?
16, 24, 32, 40, 48 ______

21. Each package of rolls contains 8 rolls. Ted bought 6 packages. How many rolls did he buy in all?

A 42 **B** 48 **C** 49 **D** 54

Name ____________________

Practice 6-5

11 and 12 as Factors

Use patterns to find each product.

1. $4 \times 11 =$ ______ **2.** $6 \times 11 =$ ______ **3.** $9 \times 11 =$ ______ **4.** $5 \times 11 =$ ______

$4 \times 12 =$ ______ $6 \times 12 =$ ______ $9 \times 12 =$ ______ $5 \times 12 =$ ______

5. 11×8 **6.** 12×10 **7.** 11×11 **8.** 12×11 **9.** 12×12

10. A dozen is another way of saying 12. How many eggs are there in a package of two dozen?

______

11. A soccer team has 11 players. There are 8 teams playing. How many people are playing soccer?

______

12. There are 6 volleyball games being played in the gym. Each game has a total of 12 players. How many people are playing volleyball in all?

______

13. Strategy Practice Maureen runs 6 miles each day. Eileen runs 9 miles each day. How many more miles does Eileen run than Maureen in 11 days?

______

14. Explain It How can you use a pattern to find the product of 5×12?

______

______

______

______

15. A jury has 12 people on it. There are enough citizens for 7 juries. How many people are there all together?

A 70

B 77

C 84

D 91

Name ______________________________

Practice
6-6

Multiplying with 3 Factors

Find the product. You may draw a picture to help.

1. $2 \times 3 \times 3$ ______

2. $2 \times 2 \times 4$ ______

3. $8 \times 2 \times 2$ ______

4. $6 \times 2 \times 3$ ______

5. $3 \times 3 \times 4$ ______

6. $5 \times 2 \times 5$ ______

7. $5 \times 4 \times 2$ ______

8. $4 \times 2 \times 3$ ______

Find the missing number.

9. $4 \times 4 \times 3 = 48$,
so $4 \times (4 \times 3) = \square$

11. Sarah and Amanda each have 2 bags with 4 marbles in each. How many marbles do they have altogether?

______

13. **Reasonableness** Is the product of $6 \times 2 \times 4$ less than 50? Explain.

____

____

14. Which number makes this number sentence true?

$8 \times 2 \times 4 = 8 \times (\blacksquare \times 4)$

A 2 **B** 4 **C** 8 **D** 64

15. Write three ways to find $3 \times 2 \times 4$.

____

____

Name ______________________________

Practice **6-7**

Problem Solving: Multiple-Step Problems

Use the pictures for **1** through **4**.

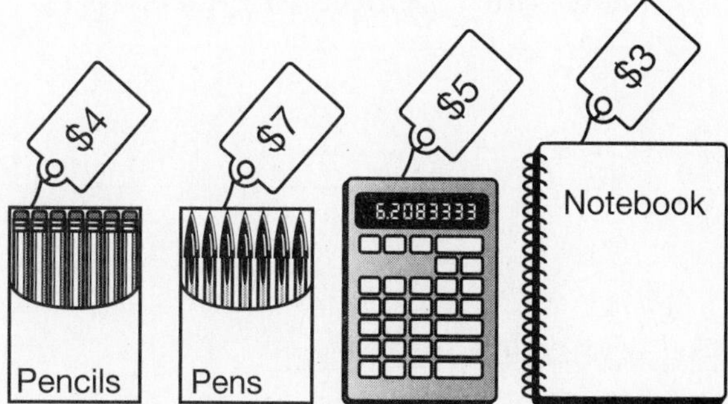

1. Teri bought 3 boxes of pencils. She paid with a $20 bill. How much change did she receive?

Tip First find the cost of the pencils.

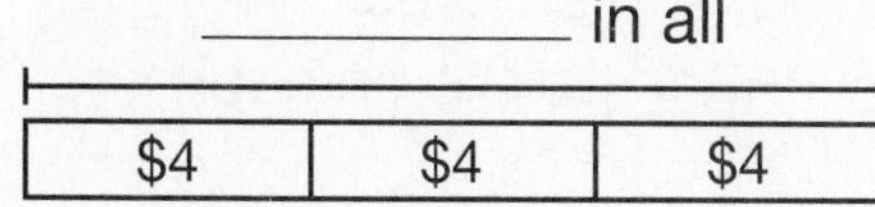

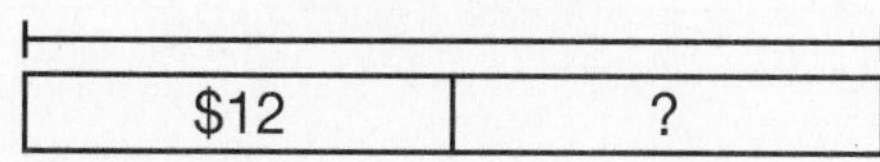

____

2. Martin bought 3 boxes of pens and a calculator. How much money did he spend all together?

Tip First find the cost of the pens.

____

3. Joey bought 2 notebooks and 2 boxes of pencils. How much money did he spend all together?

____

4. Allie bought 3 notebooks and 2 boxes of pens. She paid with $40. How much change did she receive?

____

5. Write a Problem Write a real-world problem involving multiple steps. Then solve your problem.

____

____

____

____

6. Number Sense Bert has $50 in his wallet. Then he buys 2 CDs for $13 each. How much money does he have left?

A $12 **B** $24 **C** $26 **D** $37

Name ______________________

Division as Sharing

Use counters or draw a picture to solve.

1. 24 people, 4 rows
   How many people in each row?

   ______

2. 18 marbles, 2 people
   How many marbles for each person?

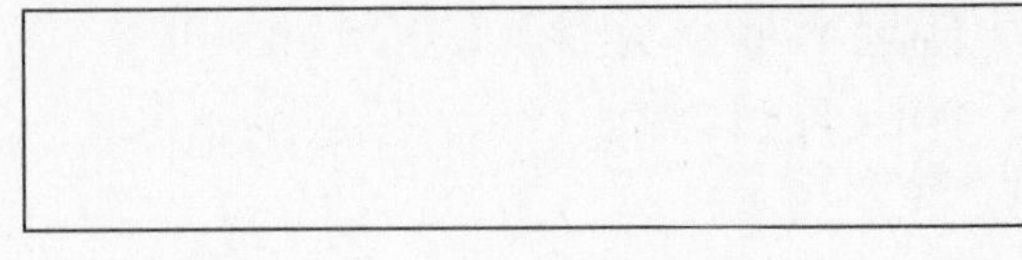

   ______

3. 25 apples, 5 trees
   How many apples on each tree?

   ______

4. 21 books, 3 shelves
   How many books on each shelf?

   ______

Complete each division sentence.

5. 15

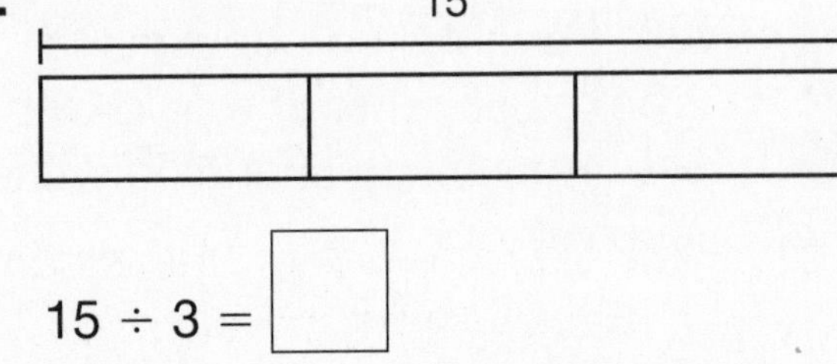

$15 \div 3 = \square$

6. 16

$16 \div 4 = \square$

7. **Explain It** Ron and Pam each have 20 pennies. Ron will put his pennies into 4 groups. Pam will put her pennies into 5 groups. Who will have more pennies in each group? Explain.

____

____

8. There are 28 days in February. There are 7 days in a week. How many weeks are there in February?

   A 3 **B** 4 **C** 5 **D** 6

Name ____________________

Practice
7-2

Understanding Remainders

Use counters or draw a picture to find each number of groups and the number left over.

1. 15 cards
4 cards in each envelope

$15 \div 4 = \square$ with $\square$ left over

2. 17 books
5 books in each box

$17 \div 5 = \square$ with $\square$ left over

3. 25 marbles
6 marbles in each bag

$25 \div 6 = \square$ with $\square$ left over

4. 22 photos
3 photos on each page

How many pages can be filled?

____

5. 14 DVDs
5 DVDs on each shelf

How many DVDs will be put on the third shelf?

____

6. 27 postcards
5 postcards in each pile

How many postcards are in the sixth pile?

____

7. $17 \div 2 = \square$ with $\square$ left over

8. $26 \div 8 = \square$ with $\square$ left over

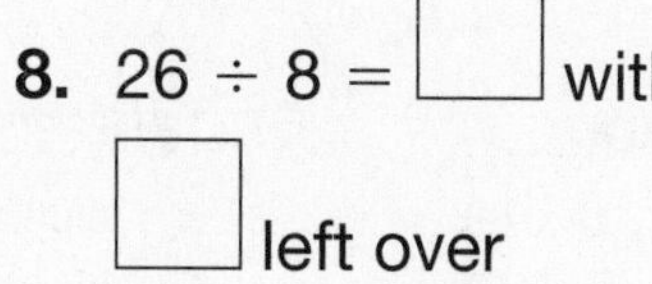

9. $34 \div 7 = \square$ with $\square$ left over

10. **Explain It** There are 25 students in Ms. Morris's class. She wants to divide the class into 3, 4, or 5 equal teams. Which number of teams can she have? Explain.

____

____

11. How many complete teams can be made with 18 people and 4 people on each team?

A 4

B 5

C 6

D 14

12. There are 14 girls trying out for cheerleading. Each team will have 6 cheerleaders. How many girls will not make a team?

____

13. **Reasoning** The Wolfpack team has 26 players. Team members will travel to their next game in cars. Each car can hold 4 players. How many cars are needed?

____

Name ______________________

Practice
7-3

Division as Repeated Subtraction

Use counters or draw a picture to solve.

1. 18 pens
3 pens in each box
How many boxes?

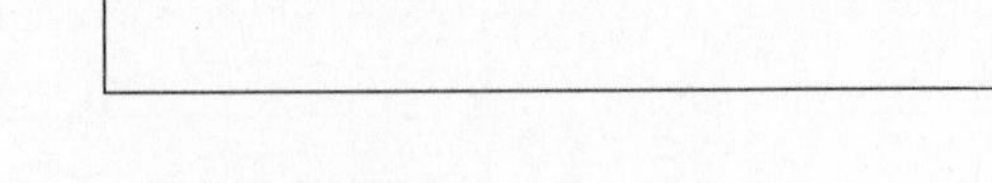

______

2. 24 students
3 students on each team
How many teams?

______

3. 35 stickers
5 stickers on each sheet
How many sheets?

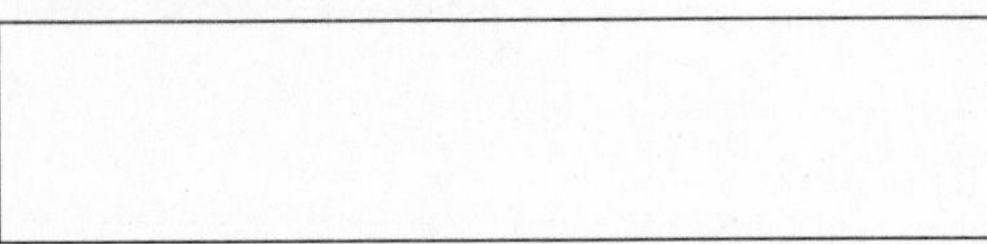

______

4. 30 leaves
6 leaves painted on each vase
How many vases?

______

5. **Number Sense** What division sentence means the same as the following subtraction sentences?

$12 - 4 = 8$
$8 - 4 = 4$
$4 - 4 = 0$

______

6. Tandem bicycles are ridden by 2 people. If 14 people rented tandem bicycles, how many bicycles were rented?

______

7. **Explain It** Tamara says that $15 \div 3 = 5$. Is she correct? Explain.

______

______

______

8. Keisha has to carry 32 boxes to her room. She can carry 4 boxes on each trip. How many trips will she take?

A 6 **B** 7 **C** 8 **D** 9

Name ______________________

Practice
7-4

Writing Division Stories

Write a division story for each number sentence.
Then use counters or draw a picture to solve.

1. 54 ÷ 6 = ☐

2. 36 ÷ 9 = ☐

3. 42 ÷ 7 = ☐

4. 25 ÷ 5 = ☐

5. There are 40 relatives at a party. There are 5 tables that each seat the same number of people. How many people can sit at each table?

6. A softball pitcher needs to get 3 outs in an inning. If a pitcher gets 21 outs, how many innings did she pitch?

7. **Explain It** There are 16 people at a party. They want to set up relay teams with exactly 3 people each. Can they do it? Explain.

8. Which division sentence will give an answer that is not in equal groups?

A 26 ÷ 4 **B** 35 ÷ 7 **C** 42 ÷ 6 **D** 45 ÷ 5

Name ____________________

Practice
7-5

Problem Solving: Use Objects and Draw a Picture

Solve. Use objects or draw a picture.

1. Ron painted part of a tiled section of his bathroom floor. The whole section was shaped like a rectangle. There were 35 square tiles in the section. How many tiles were in each row?

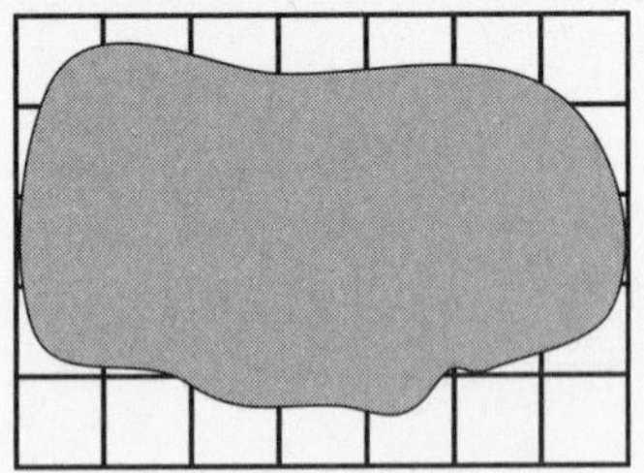

____

2. Some syrup spilled on a checkerboard-style table. The syrup covered some of the tiles. There were 36 squares on the table. How many of the squares had syrup on them?

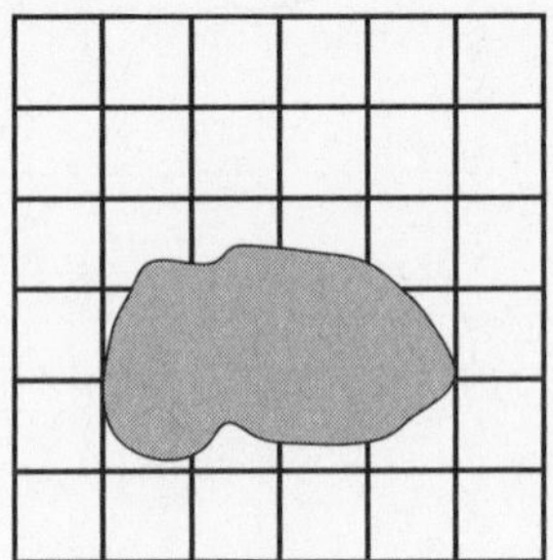

____

3. Dress rehearsal of the play was attended by 142 people. Opening night was attended by 238 people. How many people saw the two shows in all?

_______ people in all

142	238

4. Carol and Deanna drove 320 miles altogether this weekend. They drove 196 miles Sunday. How many miles did they drive Saturday?

320 miles in all

	196

5. **Write a Problem** Write and solve a real-world problem that you can solve by using objects or drawing a picture.

____

____

Name ______________________

Practice 8-1

Relating Multiplication and Division

Complete. Use counters or draw a picture to help.

1. $5 \times \square = 15$

   $15 \div 5 = \square$

2. $6 \times \square = 24$

   $24 \div 6 = \square$

3. $7 \times \square = 35$

   $35 \div 7 = \square$

4. $5 \times \square = 25$

   $25 \div 5 = \square$

5. $3 \times \square = 12$

   $12 \div 3 = \square$

6. $3 \times \square = 27$

   $27 \div 3 = \square$

7. **Number Sense** Write a fact family for 3, 6, and 18.

____

____

8. Patrick purchased 12 books. He needed 4 books for each of his projects at school. How many projects did he have?

______

9. **Draw a Picture** Draw an array. Then write a fact family to describe your array.

____

____

10. **Explain It** Evan told his class that the people in his family have 14 legs altogether. Quinton said that there must be 7 people in Evan's family. Is Quinton correct? Explain.

____

____

11. Which number makes this number sentence true? $\blacksquare \div 6 = 8$

A 2 **B** 14 **C** 24 **D** 48

Name ______________________

Practice
8-2

Fact Families with 2, 3, 4, and 5

Find each quotient.

1. 14 ÷ 2 ______ **2.** 12 ÷ 3 ______ **3.** 16 ÷ 4 ______ **4.** 30 ÷ 5 ______ **5.** 21 ÷ 3 ______

6. $2\overline{)20}$ **7.** $4\overline{)32}$ **8.** $5\overline{)40}$ **9.** $3\overline{)18}$ **10.** $4\overline{)32}$

11. Find 18 divided by 3. ______ **12.** Divide 60 by 6. ______ **13.** Find 35 divided by 5. ______

Algebra Find each missing number.

14. 45 ÷ ☐ = 5 **15.** 30 ÷ 3 = ☐ **16.** ☐ ÷ 2 = 7

Number Sense Write < or > to compare.

17. 5 × 2 ◯ 8 ÷ 2 **18.** 3 × 6 ◯ 6 ÷ 3 **19.** 4 + 8 ◯ 4 × 8

20. Gabriella and 4 friends shared a pack of 15 glue sticks equally. How many glue sticks did each person get?

______

21. Erica counted 45 fingers when the students were asked who wants to play kickball. How many hands went up?

______

22. **Explain It** Franklin says that if he divides 50 by 5, he will get 10. Jeff says he should get 9. Who is correct? Explain.

____

____

23. Which fact does not belong in the same fact family as 24 ÷ 4 = 6?

A 4 × 6 = 24 **B** 6 + 4 = 10 **C** 24 ÷ 6 = 4 **D** 6 × 4 = 24

Name ____________________

Fact Families with 6 and 7

Find each quotient.

1. $24 \div 6$ ______ **2.** $42 \div 7$ ______ **3.** $36 \div 4$ ______ **4.** $63 \div 7$ ______ **5.** $40 \div 5$ ______

6. $6\overline{)48}$ **7.** $7\overline{)49}$ **8.** $2\overline{)12}$ **9.** $6\overline{)36}$ **10.** $3\overline{)27}$

11. Find 70 divided by 7. ______ **12.** Divide 66 by 6. ______ **13.** Find 48 divided by 6. ______

14. **Explain It** How can you use a multiplication fact to find a division fact?

____

____

15. Sierra's karate class lasts 56 days.
How many weeks does the class last? ______

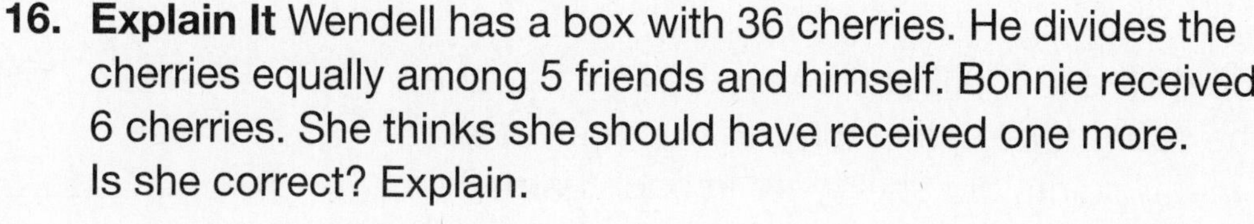

16. **Explain It** Wendell has a box with 36 cherries. He divides the cherries equally among 5 friends and himself. Bonnie received 6 cherries. She thinks she should have received one more. Is she correct? Explain.

____

____

____

17. Mr. Kline brought 30 boxes of fruit juice to a soccer game. Fruit juice comes in packages of 6. How many packages did Mr. Kline bring? ______

18. Katie bought 42 baseball cards. The cards come in packs of 7. How many packs of cards did Katie buy?

A 5 **B** 6 **C** 7 **D** 8

Name ____________________

Practice
8-4

Fact Families with 8 and 9

Find each quotient.

1. 48 ÷ 8 ____ **2.** 18 ÷ 9 ____ **3.** 49 ÷ 7 ____ **4.** 64 ÷ 8 ____ **5.** 45 ÷ 9 ____

6. $6\overline{)42}$ **7.** $8\overline{)72}$ **8.** $9\overline{)36}$ **9.** $5\overline{)15}$ **10.** $8\overline{)56}$

11. Find 81 divided by 9. ____ **12.** Divide 40 by 8. ____ **13.** Find 90 divided by 9. ____

Algebra Write < or > to compare.

14. 63 ÷ 9 ◯ 8 **15.** 32 ÷ 8 ◯ 8 **16.** 54 ÷ 9 ◯ 5

17. Reasoning It costs $7 for a matinee and $8 for an evening movie. With $56, would you be able to buy more matinee tickets or evening tickets? Explain.

____

____

18. Teri scored 64 points in the first 8 basketball games she played in. She scored the same number of points in each game. How many points did she score in each game? ____

19. Explain It Adam made 19 paper cranes Monday and 8 more Tuesday. He gave 9 friends an equal number of cranes. How many cranes did each friend receive? Explain how you found your answer.

____

____

____

20. A short story consists of 81 pages. Andrea will read 9 pages each day. How many days will it take Andrea to finish the story?

A 6 **B** 7 **C** 8 **D** 9

Name ______________________

Dividing with 0 and 1

Find each quotient.

1. $0 \div 6$ ______
2. $8 \div 8$ ______
3. $6 \div 1$ ______
4. $0 \div 5$ ______
5. $9 \div 9$ ______

6. $1\overline{)5}$
7. $4\overline{)0}$
8. $6\overline{)6}$
9. $1\overline{)8}$
10. $1\overline{)3}$

11. $3\overline{)24}$
12. $6\overline{)42}$
13. $8\overline{)72}$
14. $5\overline{)30}$
15. $7\overline{)63}$

16. Find 0 divided by 2. ______
17. Divide 7 by 1. ______
18. Find 4 divided by 4. ______

Algebra Write $<$, $>$, or $=$ to compare.

19. $6 \div 6$ ◯ $8 \div 8$
20. $0 \div 5$ ◯ $5 \div 5$
21. $9 \div 1$ ◯ $7 \div 1$

22. Tickets for rides cost $1 each at the fair. Bob has $6 to buy tickets. How many tickets can Bob buy? ______

23. **Reasoning** Nikki is the goalie on her soccer team. She has allowed 0 goals in 8 games. How many goals has she allowed in each game? ______

24. **Explain It** Why is $10 - 0 = 10$, but $0 \div 10 = 0$? Explain.

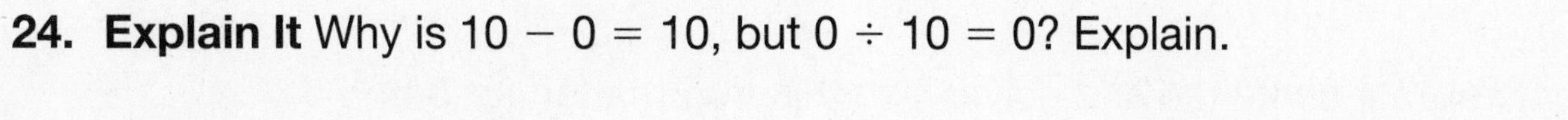

____

____

____

25. Which has the greatest quotient?

A $6 \div 6$ **B** $5 \div 1$ **C** $0 \div 3$ **D** $8 \div 8$

Name ______________________

Practice
8-6

Problem Solving: Draw a Picture and Write a Number Sentence

In **1** and **2**, draw a diagram to show what you know. Then write a number sentence and solve.

1. Maria bought 5 cans of tennis balls. Each can contained 3 tennis balls. How many tennis balls did Maria buy altogether?

____

2. In Ms. Ramirez's class, there are 28 students. They sit in 4 rows. How many students are in each row?

____

In **3** and **4**, use the chart.

Players on Team	
Sport	**Players**
Tennis	2
Basketball	5
Softball	10

3. A community center has 3 tennis teams and 5 basketball teams. No one is on both teams. How many athletes are there?

____

4. **Number Sense** Fabio said that there are 3 times as many people on a basketball team as on a tennis team. Is he correct? Explain why or why not.

____

____

____

Write a number sentence and solve. Use this information for **5** and **6**.

Marshall sleeps 8 hours each day.

5. How many hours does Marshall sleep in one week? ______________

6. How many hours is Marshall awake each day? ______________

7. Tricia spent $12 to rent ice skates. She rented them for 4 hours. Which number sentence can you write to find how much it costs to rent skates for one hour?

A $12 − $4 = ■ **B** $12 + $4 = ■ **C** $12 × $4 = ■ **D** $12 ÷ $4 = ■

Name ___________________

Practice
9-1

Repeating Patterns

Draw the next three shapes to continue the pattern.

1. 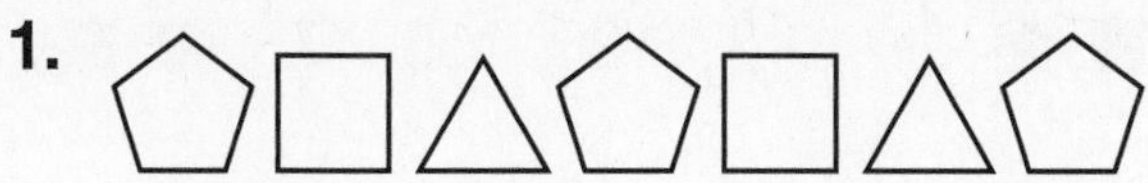

____

2. 

____

Write the next three numbers to continue the pattern.

3. 4, 6, 2, 8, 4, 6, 2, 8, 4, ...

____

4. 3, 3, 5, 3, 3, 5, 3, 3, 5, ...

____

5. **Draw a Picture** What is the 12th shape in the pattern below?

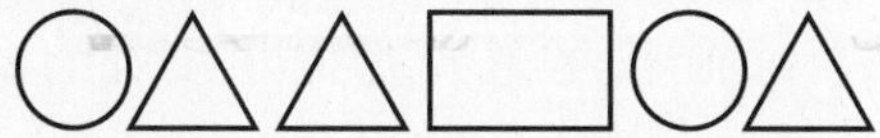

____

6. **Strategy Practice** Penny has made a pattern of shapes on her bedroom walls. She drew a rectangle, 2 circles, a rectangle, and then 2 more circles until she drew 24 circles. How many shapes did she draw in all?

____

7. Mrs. Washington placed students in a line. The order was 1 boy, 2 girls, 2 boys, and continued. Was the 10th student a boy or a girl?

____

8. What is the 15th number in the pattern below?
3, 6, 5, 2, 3, 6, 5, 2, ...

A 2 **B** 3 **C** 5 **D** 6

Name ______________________________

Practice
9-2

Number Sequences

Find the missing numbers in each pattern. Write a rule for the pattern.

1. 19, 23, 27, ■, ■

____

2. 32, 26, 20, ■, ■

____

3. 125, 150, 175, ■, ■

____

4. 8, 15, ■, ■, 36

____

5. 90, 80 ■, ■, 50

____

6. 84, 69, 54, ■, ■

____

7. 30, 50, ■, 90, ■

____

8. 65, 56, ■, 38, ■

____

9. 35, ■, 57, 68, ■

____

10. Reasoning The house numbers on Carr Memorial Avenue follow a pattern. The first four houses on the left side of the street are numbered 8, 14, 20, and 26. How many more houses are on the left side of the street with numbers less than 50?

____

11. Noreen is beginning an exercise program. The first week she exercises 25 minutes each day. The second week she exercises 30 minutes a day and the third week she increases it to 35 minutes a day. If the pattern continues, how long will she exercise each day in the fifth week?

____

12. Explain It What do you need to do to extend a pattern?

____

____

____

13. John said that 52 is part of the pattern below. Mary said that 66 is part of the pattern below. Who is correct?
18, 26, 34, 42, …

A Neither is correct.
B Both are correct.
C Only John is correct.
D Only Mary is correct.

Name ______________________

Practice 9-3

Extending Tables

Find the missing numbers.

1.

Number of Cats	Number of Legs
1	4
2	
3	12
4	16
	32

2.

Money Earned	Money Saved
$25	$15
$32	$22
$43	
	$47
$73	$63

3.

Touchdowns	Points
1	6
2	12
3	
	36
8	48

For **4** and **5**, use the table at the right.

T-shirts	Cost
1	$8
3	$24
5	$40

4. How much money would 9 T-shirts cost?

____

5. **Strategy Practice** How much more money do 10 T-shirts cost than 6 T-shirts? Explain how you determined your answer.

____

____

____

6. **Number Sense** Bob has 3 bookshelves that hold a total of 27 books. He adds a fourth shelf and now has 36 books. If he adds 2 more shelves, how many books can he have in total?

____

7. What is the missing number in the table below?

In	3	5	8	15
Out	9	11	14	

A 21 **B** 25 **C** 30 **D** 45

Name ___________________________

Practice
9-4

Writing Rules for Situations

Find the missing numbers in each table.
Write a rule for the table.

1.

Max's Age	Carol's Age
7	13
10	
14	20
18	24
	31

____

2.

Tricycles	Wheels
5	15
3	9
7	
	27
2	6

____

3.

Old Price	New Price
$25	$18
$16	$9
	$32
$53	$46
$72	

____

For **4** and **5**, use the table at the right.

Players	Teams
24	4
48	8
36	6
30	5

4. The table shows the number of players on a volleyball team. What is a rule for the table?

____

5. **Explain It** If there are 12 teams, how many players will there be? Explain how you found your answer.

____

____

6. How many miles can Nick travel in 5 hours? 6 hours?

Hours	1	2	3	4
Miles	60	120	180	240

____

7. The table shows how many CDs Jim and Ken each own after joining a CD club. Which is a rule that works for this table?

Jim	8	12	20	30
Ken	16	20	28	38

A Add 8
C Subtract 8
B Multiply by 2
D Divide by 2

Name ____________________

Translating Words to Expressions

Write a numerical expression for each word phrase.

1. a total of 21 that is split into 3 equal groups
2. the difference when 9 is taken away from 24
3. the sum of 32 and 27
4. the product of 7 and 5
5. 3 times as old as 6 years old
6. 15 CDs more than 12 CDs
7. 32 carrots shared equally by 8 people
8. \$20 paid from \$50

There were 12 people on a bus. Write a numerical expression for the number of people after each action described. For each problem, start with 12 people.

9. 4 people leave the bus
10. 6 people get on the bus
11. half of the people leave the bus
12. twice as many people on the bus now
13. **Geometry** A figure has 3 more sides than a pentagon. Write an expression for the number of sides the new figure has.
14. Kim has 20 books on each of 4 shelves. Which number sentence shows how to find how many books in all?

    A $20 + 4$ **C** $20 - 4$

    B 4×20 **D** $20 \div 4$

Name ____________________

Practice
9-6

Geometric Patterns

Draw the next two figures in the pattern.
Find the missing numbers in each table.

1.

Number of Stories	1	2	3	4	5
Number of Blocks	5	10	15		

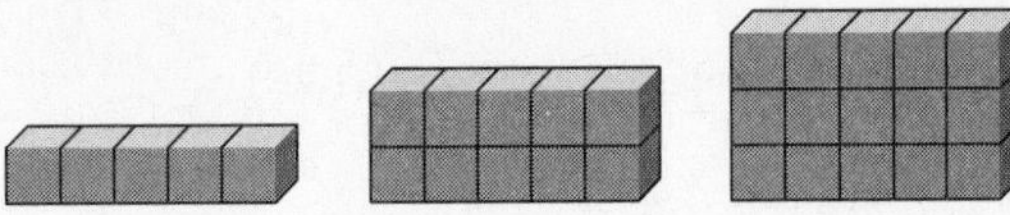

2.

Number of Stories	1	2	3	4	5
Number of Blocks	2	4	6		

3.

Length of Each Side	1	2	3	4	5
Sum of All Sides	3	6	9		

1 2 3

4.

Number of Stories	1	2	3	4	5
Number of Blocks	6	12	18		

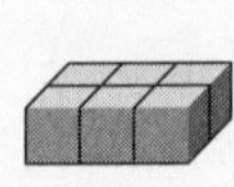

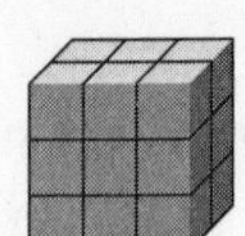

5. Explain It Use Exercise 4. How could you find how many blocks there were in 20 stories? How many blocks would there be?

6. Which is a rule for the table below?

In	3	9	4	7
Out	7	13	8	11

A Add 4

B Multiply 2

C Multiply 4

D Add 5

Name ___________________________

Practice
9-7

Equal or Unequal

Compare. Write $<$, $>$, or $=$ for each ◯.

1. $8 + 17$ ◯ 24

2. $22 + 29$ ◯ $36 + 17$

3. $44 + 12$ ◯ $62 - 6$

4. $38 + 27$ ◯ $79 - 12$

Write a number that makes each number sentence true.

5. $6 + \square = 15$

6. $23 - \square < 14$

7. $8 + \square > 14$

8. $12 - \square > 6$

9. Mr. King's and Ms. Rodney's classes are competing in field day. Mr. King's class has 12 boys and 13 girls. Ms. Rodney's class has 14 boys and 12 girls. Write a number sentence to compare the number of students.

____

10. Strategy Practice Adam has 24 U.S. stamps. Sara has 17 U.S. stamps. Adam gives Sarah 4 U.S. stamps. Write a number sentence to compare the number of U.S. stamps each has now.

____

11. Estimation Keisha has a shelf that has 38 books and another shelf that has 29 books. About how many books are on the two shelves in all?

____

12. Which symbol goes in the ◯ to compare the expressions correctly?

$31 - 15$ ◯ $9 + 6$

A $+$

B $>$

C $<$

D $=$

Name ________________________________

Practice
9-8

Problem Solving: Act It Out and Use Reasoning

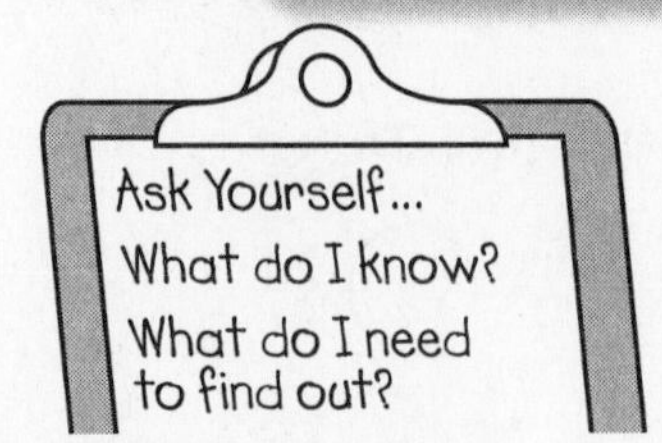

Solve. Find the number of each kind of object in the collection.

1. **Sue's Card Collection**

   8 packs of baseball cards
   3 fewer packs of hockey cards than football cards
   17 packs in all

   Baseball cards = ☐

   Hockey cards = ☐

   Football cards = ☐

2. **Drew's DVD Collection**

   7 comedy DVDs
   4 more drama DVDs than horror DVDs
   15 DVDs in all

   Comedy DVDs = ☐

   Drama DVDs = ☐

   Horror DVDs = ☐

3. **Strategy Practice** Mike is 8 years older than Kyle. Kyle is 6 years old. The sum of Mike's, Kyle's, and Jamal's ages is 23. How many years old is Jamal?

   ____

4. Miranda has 24 CDs in her collection. Of those CDs, 10 are pop CDs. She has 6 more country CDs than jazz CDs. How many country CDs does Miranda have?

   ____

5. Curt has 12 models in all. Three of the models are airplanes. Curt has 5 more models of cars than boats. How many models of cars does Curt have?

   ____

6. Stevie, Lindsey, and Christine are the lead singers in a band. They will sing 18 songs. Lindsey will sing 8 songs. Christine will sing 6 fewer songs than Stevie. How many songs will Stevie sing?

   A 2　　**B** 4　　**C** 6　　**D** 8

Name ______________________

Solid Figures

Name the solid figure.

1. 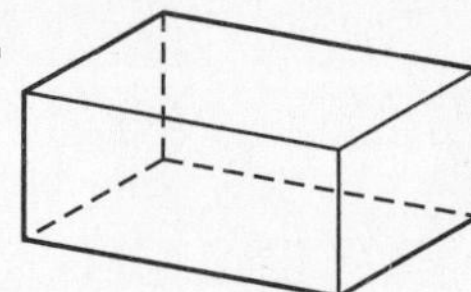
____

2. 
____

3. 
____

4. 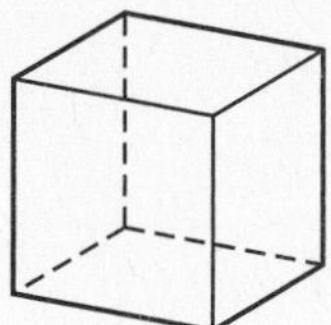
____

5. 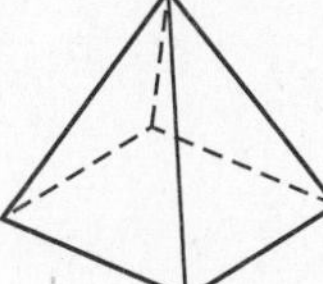
____

6. 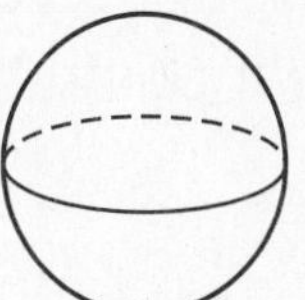
____

Name the solid figure that each object looks like.

7. 
____

8. 

____

9. 

____

10. 

____

11. **Reasoning** What solid figures would you get if you cut a cube as shown? ______________

12. What solid figure does this figure most resemble?

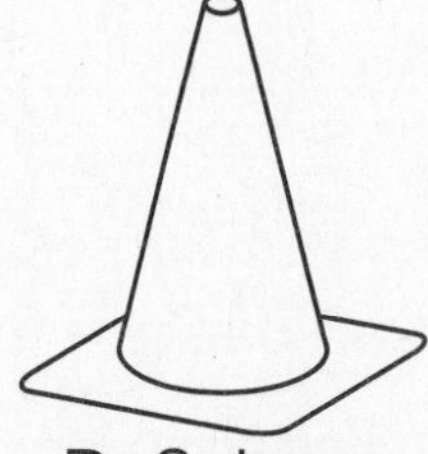

A Cylinder **B** Cone **C** Pyramid **D** Sphere

Name ______________________

Relating Solids and Shapes

For **1** through **4**, use the rectangular prism pictured at the right.

1. How many faces does this rectangular prism have?

_____

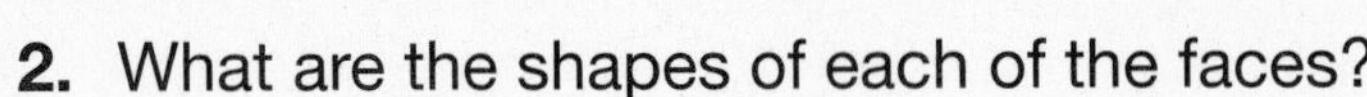

2. What are the shapes of each of the faces?

____

3. How many edges does this rectangular prism have?

_____

4. How many vertices does this rectangular prism have?

_____

For **5** through **8**, use the pyramid pictured at the right.

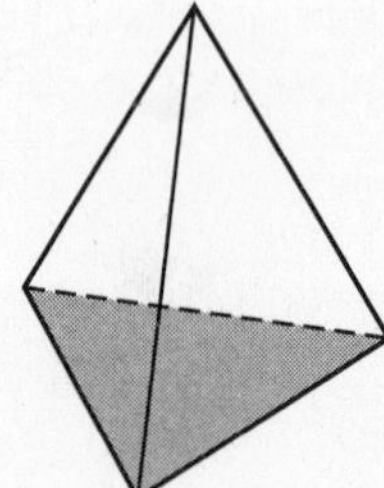

5. How many faces does this pyramid have?

_____

6. What are the shapes of each of the faces?

____

7. How many edges does this pyramid have?

_____

8. How many vertices does this pyramid have?

_____

9. Explain It How could you describe a cylinder to someone who has never seen one?

____

____

____

10. Which two figures have the same number of faces, edges, and vertices?

A Cylinder and pyramid
B Rectangular prism and sphere
C Pyramid and cube
D Rectangular prism and cube

Name ________________________

Practice
10-3

Lines and Line Segments

Write the name for each.

1.  **2.** **3.** 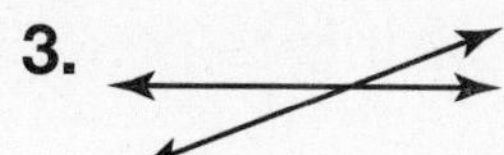 **4.**

______ ______ ______ ______

Draw and label a picture of each.

5. Parallel lines

6. Line segment

7. Intersecting lines

8. Line

For **9** and **10**, use the map at the right. Tell if the trails named look like intersecting lines or parallel lines.

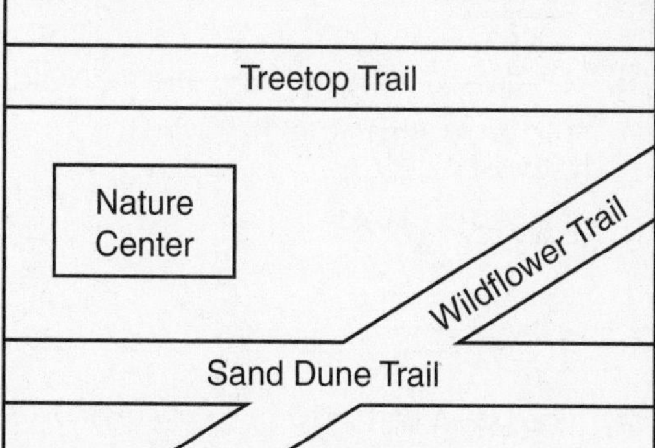

9. Treetop and Sand Dune

____

10. Sand Dune and Wildflower

____

11. Explain It What is the difference between a line and a line segment?

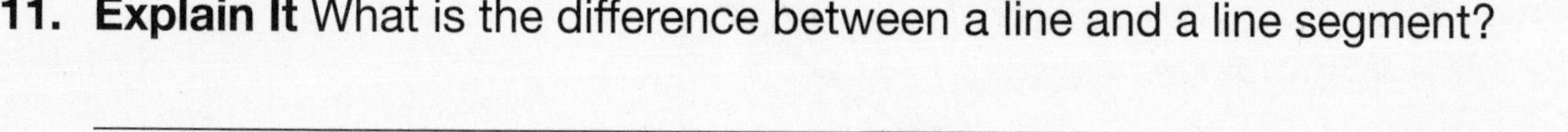

____

____

____

12. How many times does a pair of intersecting lines cross?

A Never **B** 1 time **C** 2 times **D** 3 times

Name ____________________

Practice **10-4**

Angles

Tell if each angle is right, acute, or obtuse.

1. **2.** **3.** **4.**

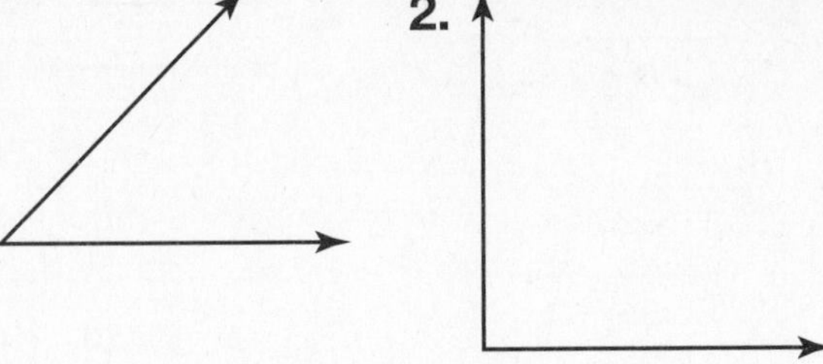

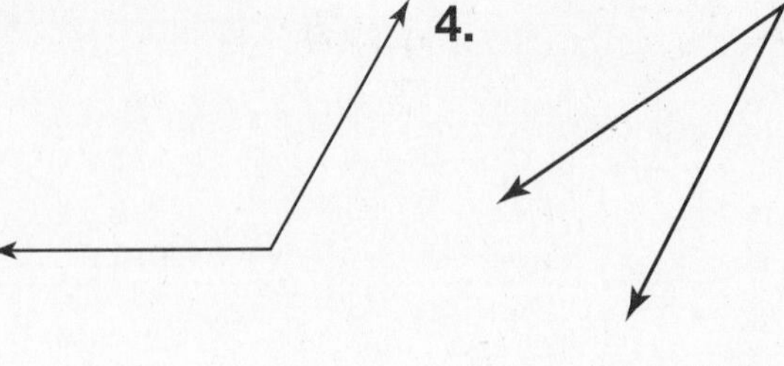

__________ __________ __________ __________

Draw and label a picture of each.

5. Acute angle

6. Ray

7. Right angle

8. Obtuse angle

9. Explain It How are perpendicular lines similar to intersecting lines? How are they different?

____

____

10. Reasoning Jill said that an angle is made of two rays. Is she correct? Explain.

____

____

11. Can parallel rays form an angle? Explain.

____

12. At what time do the hands of a clock form an acute angle?

A 2:00 **B** 4:00 **C** 6:00 **D** 8:00

Name ____________________

Practice
10-5

Polygons

Name the polygon.

1.  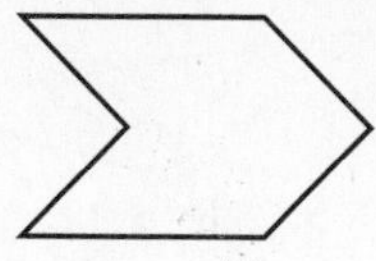 ____________

2. 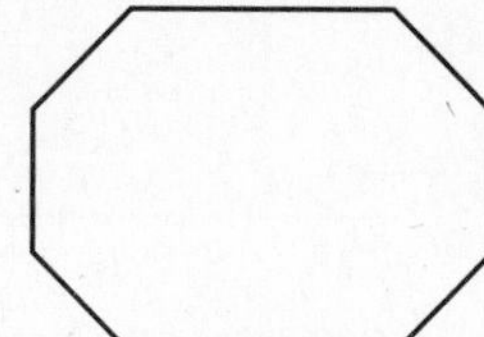 ____________

3. 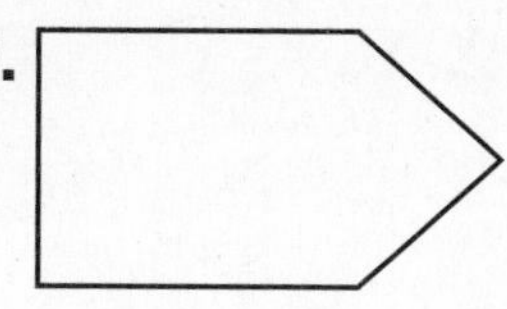 ____________

4. 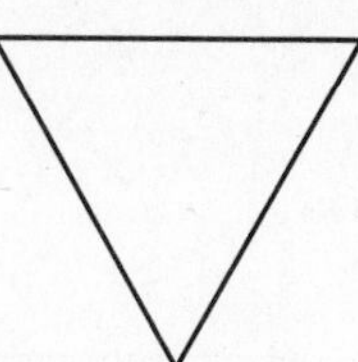 ____________

Is each figure a polygon? If it is not, explain why.

5. 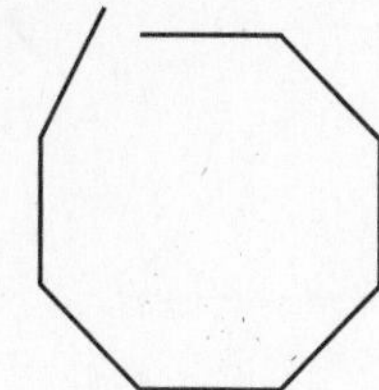 ____________

6. 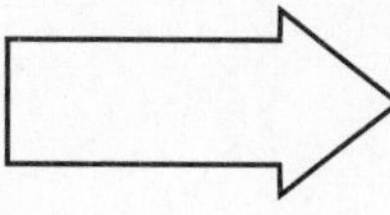 ____________

7. 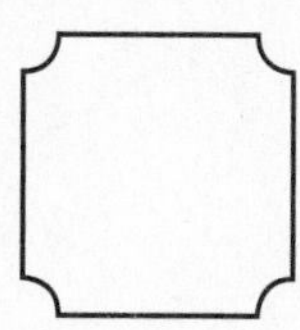 ____________

8. 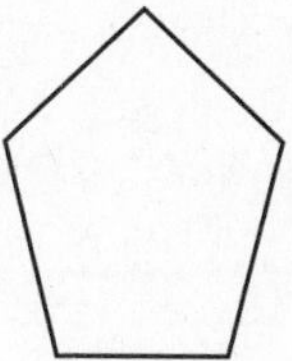 ____________

9. **Explain It** Juan said that the two figures below are quadrilaterals. Is he correct? Explain.

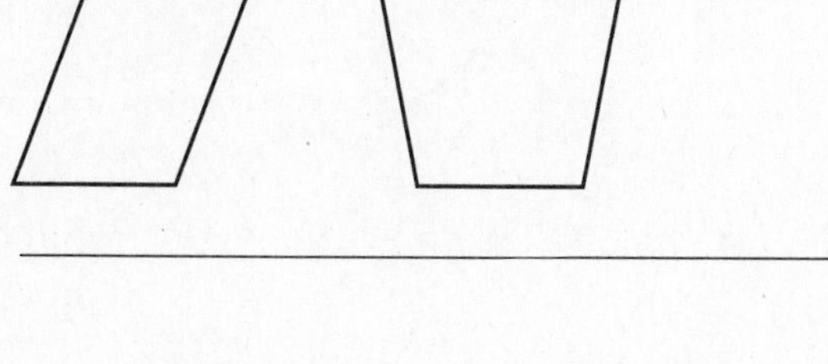

____

____

____

10. **Reasoning** If two of the line segments of a polygon are parallel, what is the least number of sides it could have?

____

11. How many more sides does an octagon have than a pentagon?

A 1 **B** 2 **C** 3 **D** 4

Name ______________________

Triangles

Tell if each triangle is equilateral, isosceles, or scalene.

1. 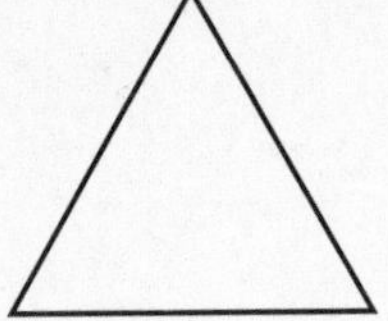 ____________

2. 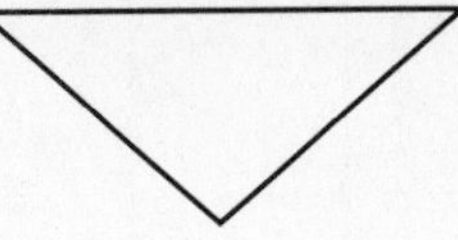 ____________

3. 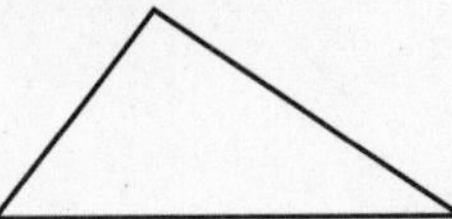 ____________

4. 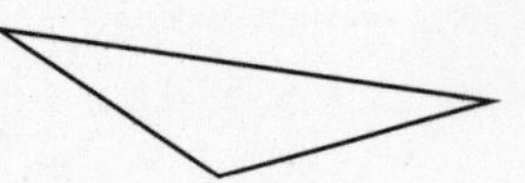 ____________

Tell if each triangle is right, acute, or obtuse.

5. 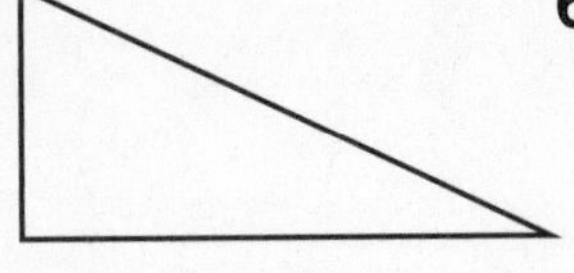 ____________

6.  ____________

7. 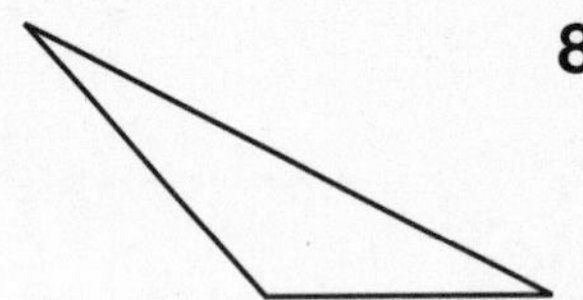 ____________

8. 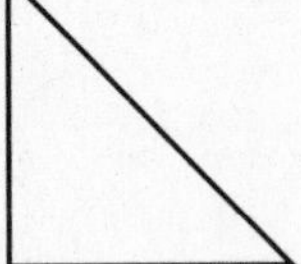 ____________

9. Explain It Can a triangle have 2 right angles? Explain.

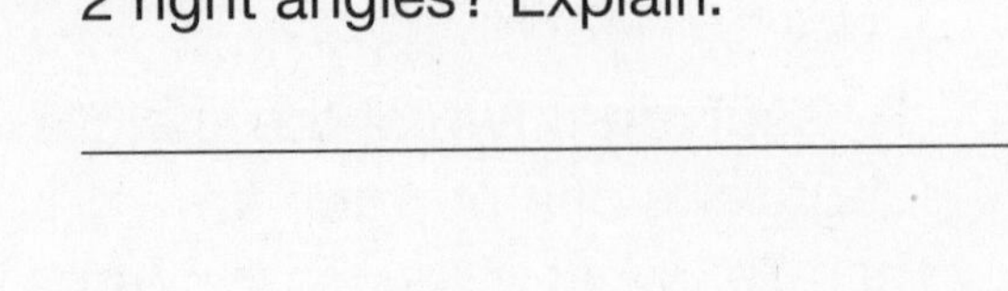

____

____

____

10. Reasoning What is the least number of acute angles that a triangle can have?

____

11. Which two types of triangles identify the figure?

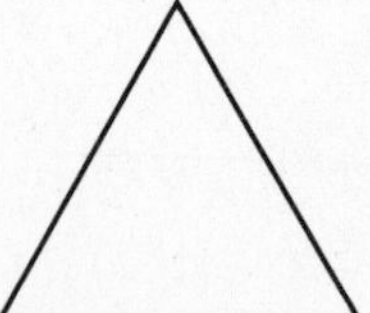

A Equilateral triangle, acute triangle

B Equilateral triangle, right triangle

C Scalene triangle, acute triangle

D Isosceles triangle, obtuse triangle

Name ________________________

Practice
10-7

Quadrilaterals

Write as many names as possible for each quadrilateral.

1. **2.** **3.** **4.** **5.**

In **6** through **9**, write the name that best describes the quadrilateral.

6. A parallelogram with 4 equal sides, but no right angles.

7. A rectangle with 4 right angles and all sides the same length.

8. A figure that is not a parallelogram, with one pair of parallel sides.

9. A parallelogram with 4 right angles and with sides different in length and width.

10. **Explain It** Can a rectangle also be a rhombus?

11. Which of the following correctly names the figure?

A Rhombus
B Trapezoid
C Parallelogram
D Rectangle

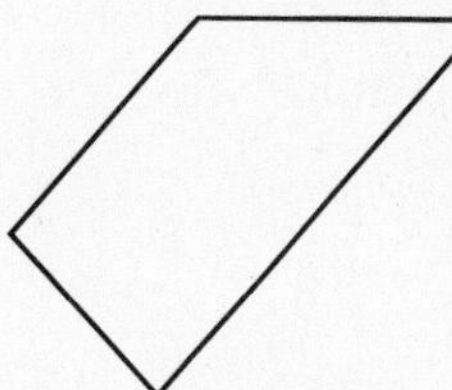

Name ____________________

Problem Solving: Make and Test Generalizations

In **1** through **4**, make a generalization for each set of polygons.

1.

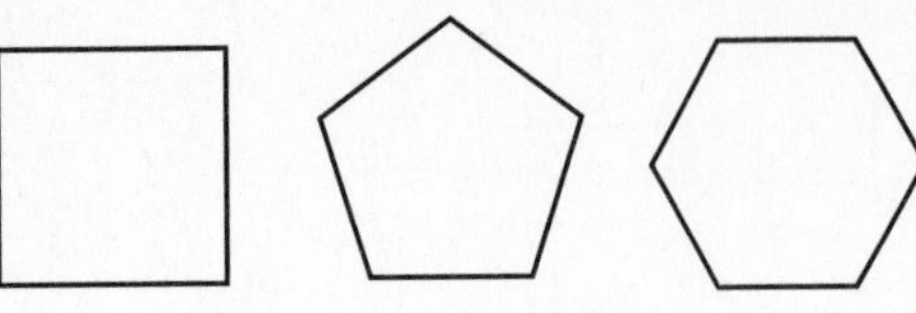

____

2.

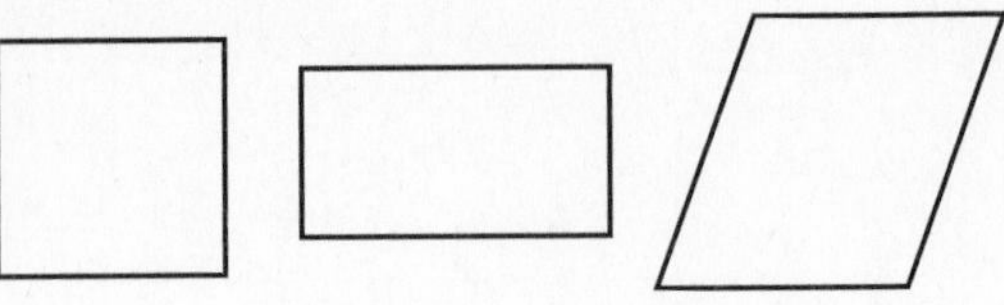

____

3.

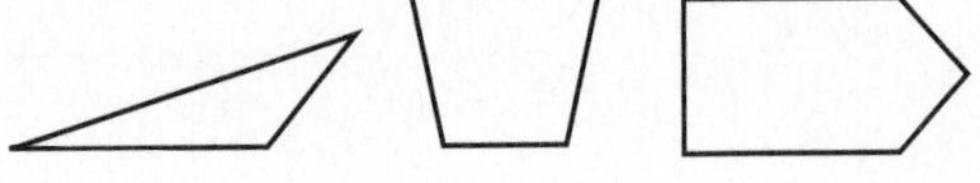

____

4.

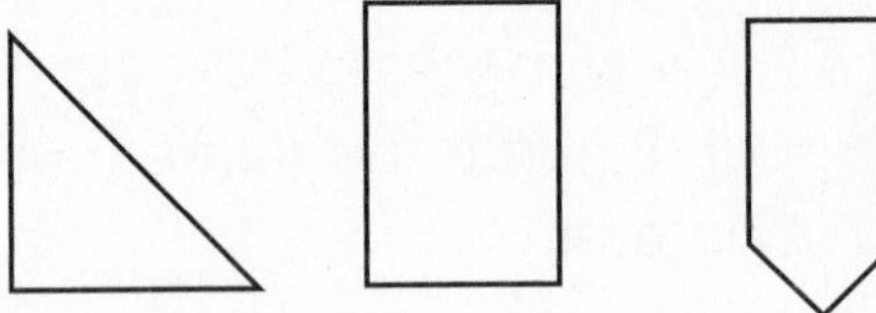

____

5. Reasoning Is this generalization true? If not, draw a picture to show why not.
All triangles have at least 2 acute angles.

____

6. What do all of these numbers have in common?

3, 5, 7, 11, 13

____

____

____

7. Number Sense Compare each quotient to its dividend.

$42 \div 6 = 7$
$8 \div 1 = 8$
$12 \div 12 = 1$

Make a generalization about dividends and quotients for whole numbers.

____

8. What is the same in all of these polygons?

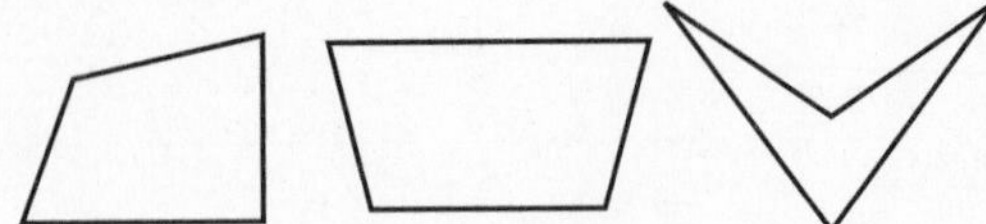

A They are all rectangles.
B They are all rhombuses.
C They are all quadrilaterals.
D They all have right angles.

Name ______________________

Practice 11-1

Congruent Figures and Motion

Write *translation, reflection,* or *rotation* for each pair of congruent figures.

1. 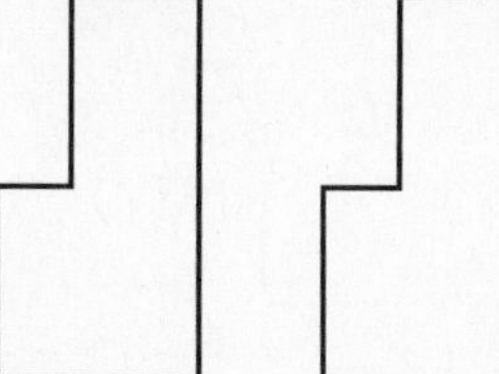

____

2. 

____

3. 

____

Are the figures congruent? Write *yes* or *no*. You may trace to decide.

4. 

____

5. 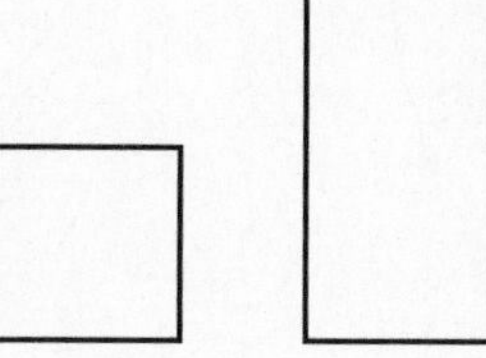

____

6. 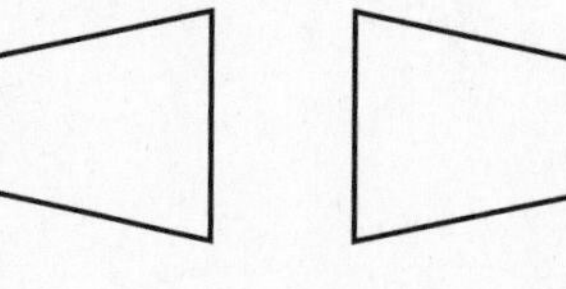

____

7. **Reasoning** Are all squares congruent? Explain.

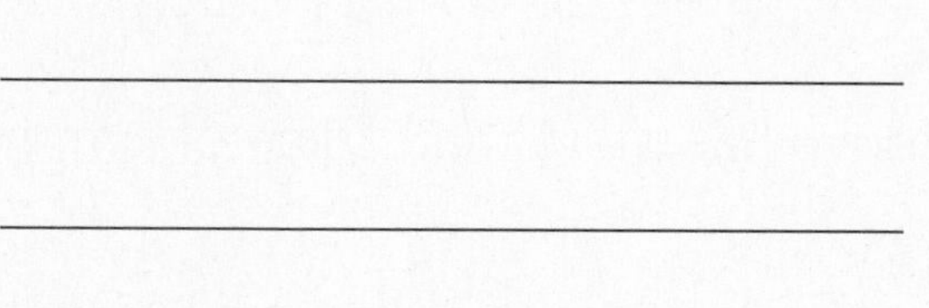

8. **Explain It** Could a triangle and a rectangle ever be congruent? Explain.

____

9. Which of the following are congruent figures?

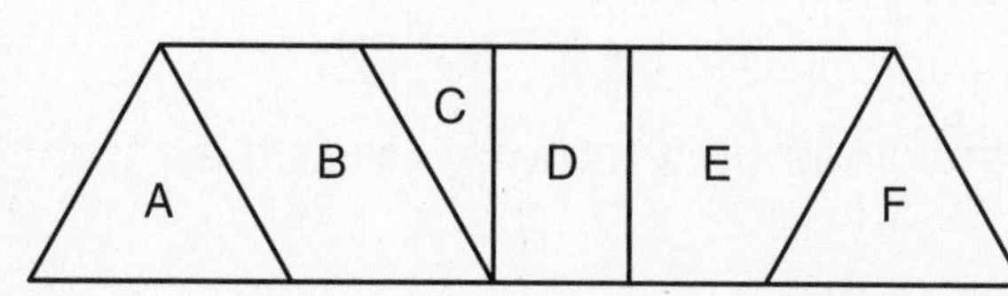

A A and E　**B** B and D　**C** C and F　**D** A and F

Name ____________________

Practice
11-2

Line Symmetry

Is the figure symmetric? Write *yes* or *no*. You may trace to decide.

1. 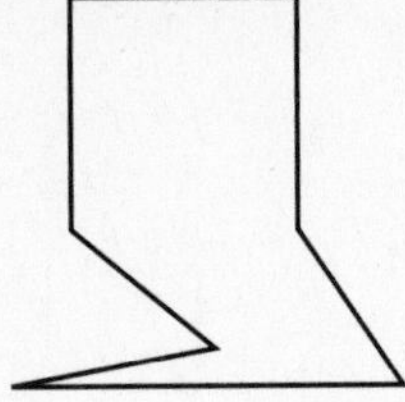 ________

2. 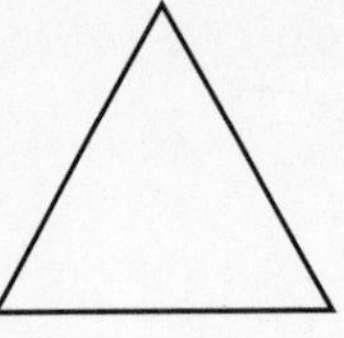 ________

3. 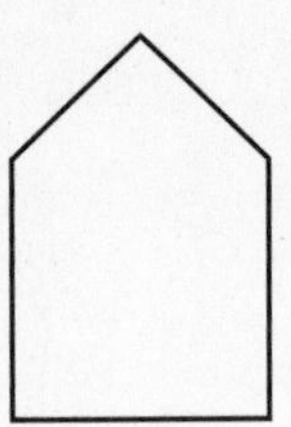 ________

4.  ________

5. 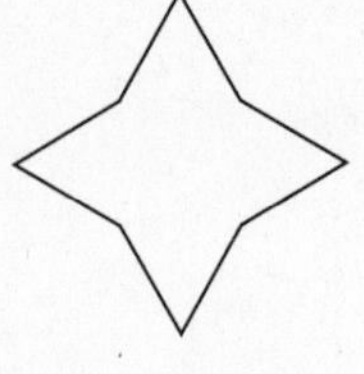 ________

6. 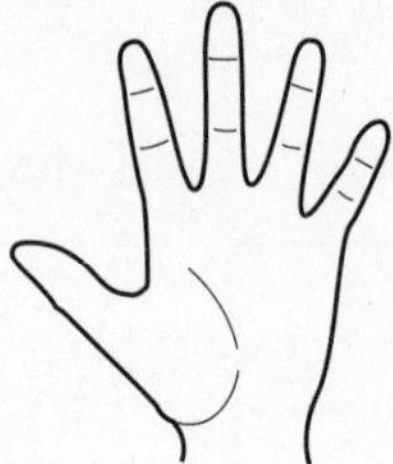 ________

7.  ________

8.  ________

9. Writing to Explain How do you know if a figure is symmetric?

____

____

____

10. Reasoning One of the figures in 1–4 above has more than 1 line of symmetry. Which figure? Explain.

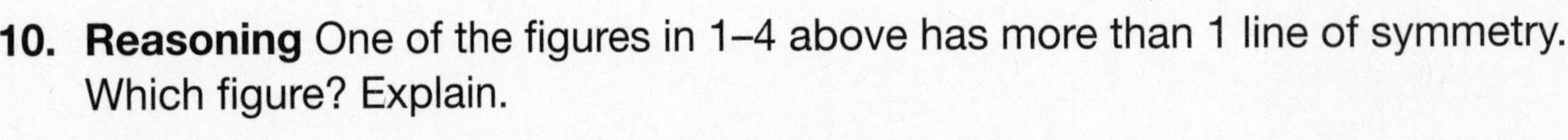

____

____

____

11. How many lines of symmetry does the rhombus to the right have?

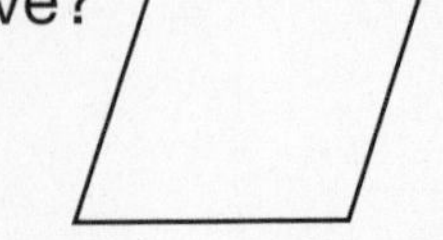

A 0 **B** 1 **C** 2 **D** 3

12. Which figures always have the same number of lines of symmetry?

A Triangles **B** Trapezoids **C** Squares **D** Pentagons

Name ______________________

Drawing Shapes with Lines of Symmetry

Complete the figure so the dashed line segment is part of a line of symmetry.

1. 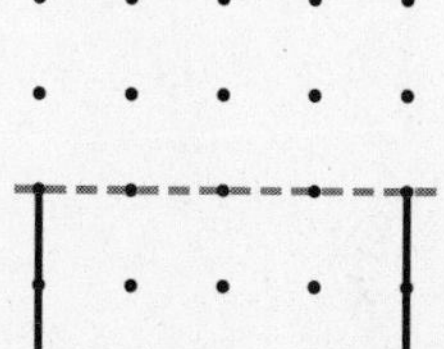

2. 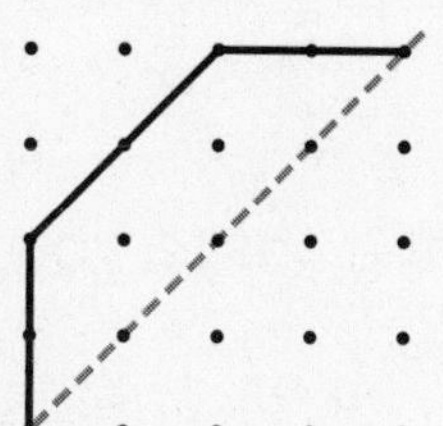

3. 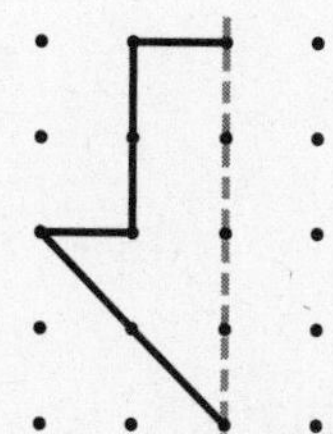

4. 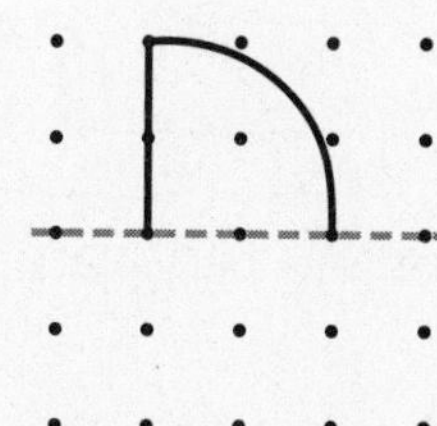

5. **Explain It** How can you use this shape to make a symmetric figure? Classify the shape created.

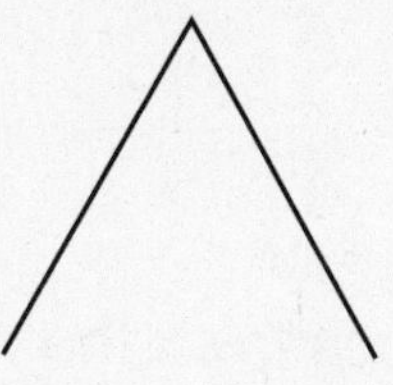

____

____

____

____

____

____

6. The dashed line is part of a line of symmetry. Which picture completes the figure?

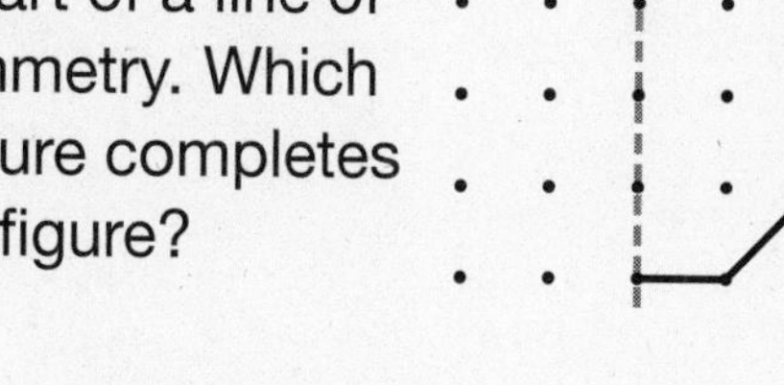

A 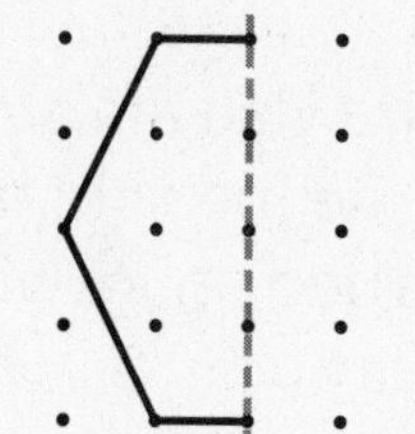

B 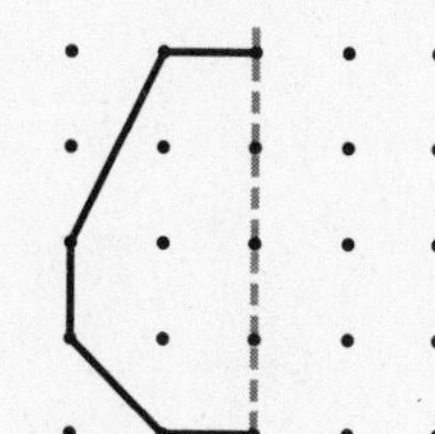

C 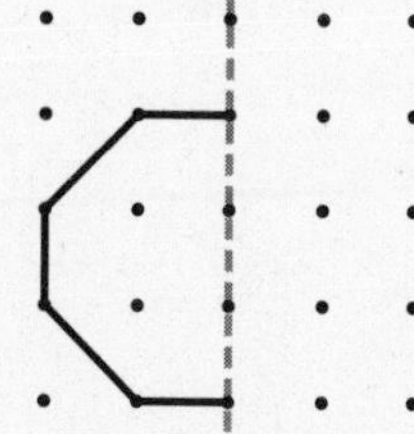

D 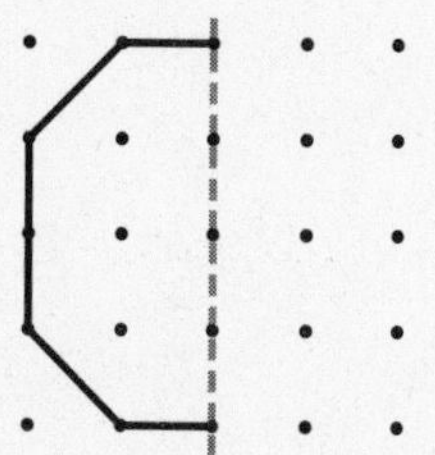

Name ______________________________

Problem Solving: Use Objects

Use the tangram to make the shape. Draw the shape you made.

1. Use the medium triangle and the two small triangles. Make a shape that has at least two lines of symmetry.

2. Use the square and the two small triangles. Make a shape that has at least two lines of symmetry.

3. **Draw a Picture** Use the two large triangles and the medium triangle to make a 5-sided figure with one line of symmetry.

4. Use any five pieces from the tangram set. Make at least three different shapes. Draw all of the shapes you made.

Name ______________________

Practice 12-1

Dividing Regions into Equal Parts

Tell if each shows equal or unequal parts. If the parts are equal, name them.

1. 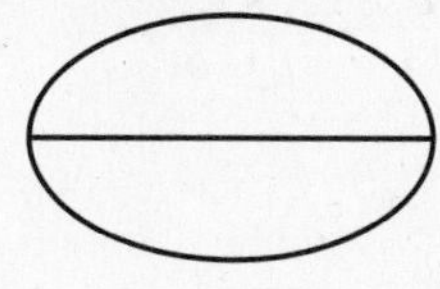

2. 

3. 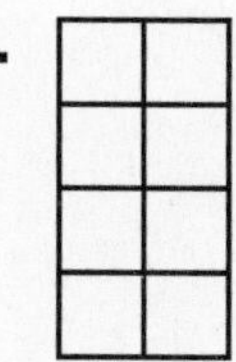

4. 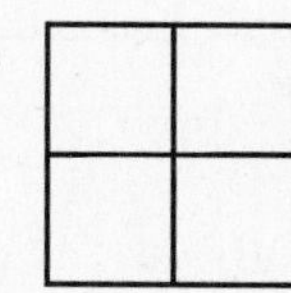

Name the equal parts of the whole.

5. 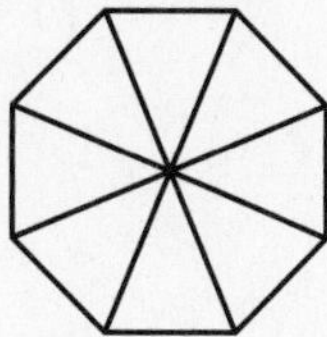

6. 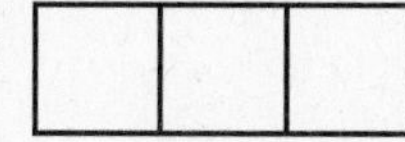

7. 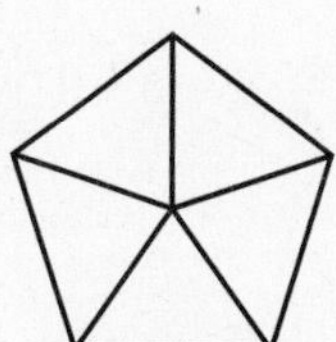

8. 

Use the grid to draw a region showing the number of equal parts named.

9. tenths

10. sixths

11. **Geometry** How many equal parts does this figure have?

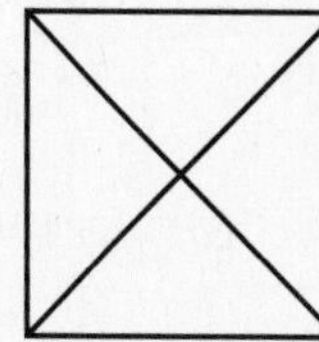

12. Which is the name of 12 equal parts of a whole?

A halves **B** sixths **C** tenths **D** twelfths

Name ______________________

Practice
12-2

Fractions and Regions

Write the fraction of each figure that is shaded.

1. 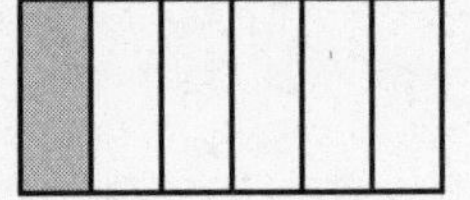 ________

2. 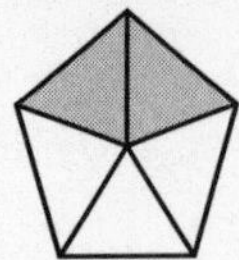 ________

3.  ________

4. 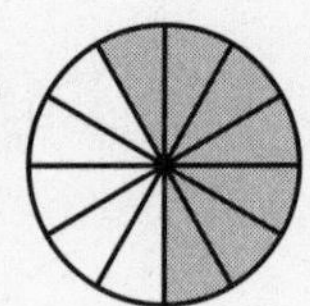 ________

Draw a picture to show each fraction.

5. $\frac{3}{8}$

6. $\frac{1}{4}$

7. $\frac{4}{5}$

In **8** and **9**, use the information below.

Three parts of a rectangle are red. Two parts are blue.

8. What fraction of the rectangle is red?

____

9. **Reasoning** What fraction of the rectangle is blue?

____

10. **Draw a Picture** A banner is made of 8 equal parts. Five of the parts contain stars. Three of the parts contain hearts. Draw the banner.

11. How can you write the fraction $\frac{4}{6}$ in word form?

A fourth sixth **B** four sixes **C** four sixths **D** fourth six

Name ___

Fractions and Sets

Practice
12-3

In **1** through **3**, write the fraction of the counters that are shaded.

1. 

___

2. 

___

3. 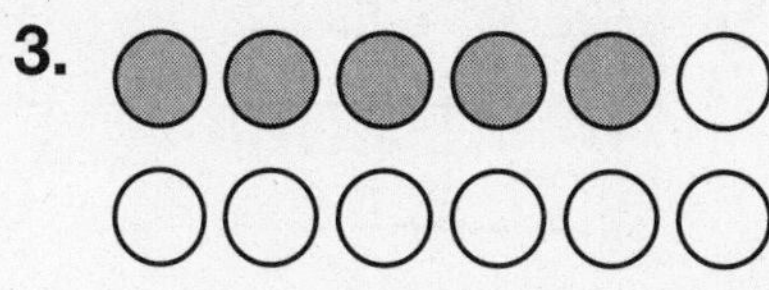

___

Draw a picture of the set described.

4. 4 shapes, $\frac{3}{4}$ of the shapes are squares

5. 6 shapes, $\frac{1}{6}$ of the shapes are circles

6. 10 shapes, $\frac{7}{10}$ of the shapes are triangles

In **7** and **8**, use the utensils to answer the questions.

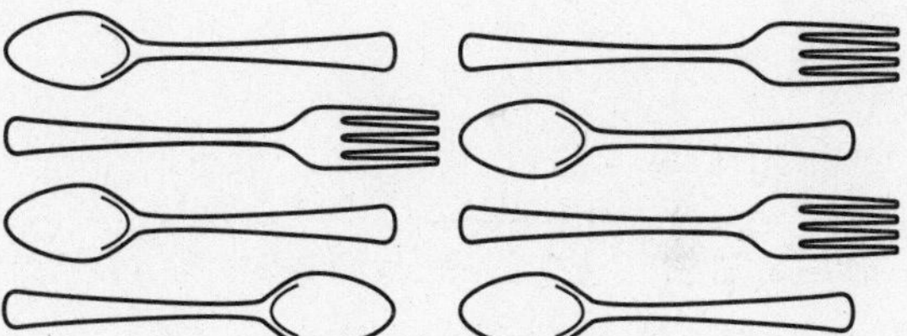

7. What fraction of the utensils are forks?

___

8. What fraction of the utensils are spoons?

___

9. **Number Sense** Johnny bought 5 movie tickets and spent \$44. Of the tickets he bought, $\frac{3}{5}$ were children's tickets that cost \$8 each. The other tickets were adult tickets. How much does one adult ticket cost?

___

10. Pamela has 4 pink ribbons, 3 green ribbons, and 2 blue ribbons. What fraction of Pamela's ribbons are green?

A $\frac{3}{9}$ **B** $\frac{3}{6}$ **C** $\frac{3}{5}$ **D** $\frac{3}{4}$

Name ______________________

Benchmark Fractions

Estimate the fractional part of each that is shaded.

1. ______________

2. ______________

3. ______________

4. ______________

What benchmark fraction is closest to each point? Choose from the benchmark fractions $\frac{1}{2}$, $\frac{1}{3}$, $\frac{2}{3}$, $\frac{1}{4}$, and $\frac{3}{4}$.

5. *E* ______________ 6. *F* ______________ 7. *G* ______________

Estimate the amount that is left.

8. 

____

9. 

____

10. 

____

11. **Draw a Picture** Draw a circle and shade it to show about $\frac{1}{3}$ shaded.

12. Which is the best estimate for the amount of the square that is shaded?

A $\frac{1}{4}$

B $\frac{1}{3}$

C $\frac{1}{2}$

D $\frac{2}{3}$

Name ______________________

Finding Equivalent Fractions

Complete each number sentence.

1. 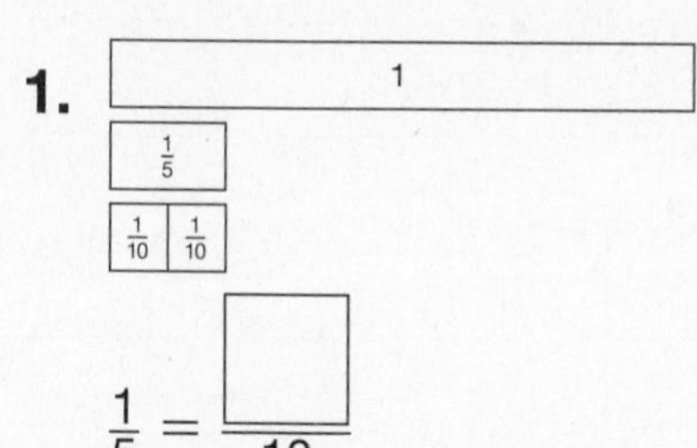

$\frac{1}{5} = \frac{\square}{10}$

2. 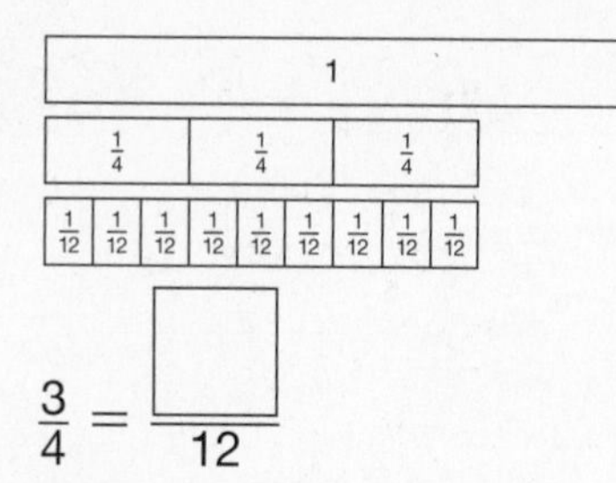

$\frac{3}{4} = \frac{\square}{12}$

3. 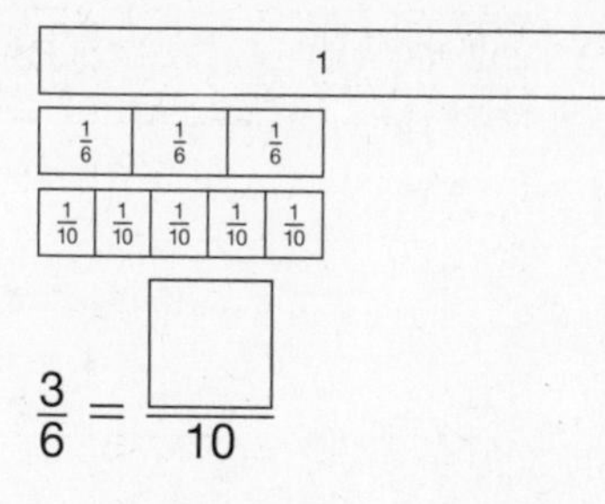

$\frac{3}{6} = \frac{\square}{10}$

Find the simplest form of each fraction.

4. $\frac{3}{12}$ ______

5. $\frac{8}{10}$ ______

6. $\frac{3}{8}$ ______

Name a fraction to solve each problem.

7. Rob colored $\frac{1}{4}$ of a rectangle. What is another way to name $\frac{1}{4}$?

____

8. Three fifths of the cast in a musical have to sing. What fraction of the cast does not have to sing?

______

Complete each pattern.

9. $\frac{1}{3}, \frac{2}{6}, \frac{3}{9}, \frac{4}{\square}$

10. $\frac{1}{2}, \frac{2}{4}, \frac{3}{6}, \frac{4}{8}, \frac{5}{\square}, \frac{6}{\square}$

11. **Explain It** When using fraction strips, how do you know that two fractions are equivalent?

____

____

____

____

____

12. Samuel has read $\frac{5}{6}$ of his assignment. Judy has read $\frac{10}{12}$ of her assignment. Their assignments were the same size. Which sentence is true?

A Samuel read more than Judy.

B Judy read more than Samuel.

C They read the same amount.

D They will both finish the assignment at the same time.

Name ______________________________

Use Models to Compare Fractions

Compare. Write >, <, or =.

1. 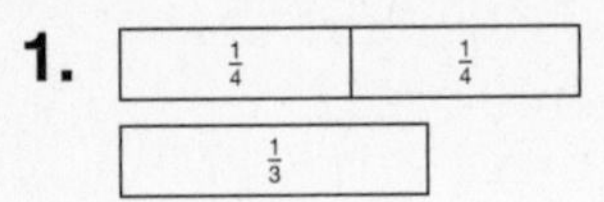

$\frac{2}{4}$ ◯ $\frac{1}{3}$

2. $\frac{1}{8}$ | $\frac{1}{8}$ | $\frac{1}{8}$

$\frac{1}{2}$

$\frac{3}{8}$ ◯ $\frac{1}{2}$

3. $\frac{1}{4}$ | $\frac{1}{4}$ | $\frac{1}{4}$

$\frac{1}{8}$ | $\frac{1}{8}$ | $\frac{1}{8}$ | $\frac{1}{8}$ | $\frac{1}{8}$ | $\frac{1}{8}$

$\frac{3}{4}$ ◯ $\frac{6}{8}$

4. $\frac{1}{5}$

$\frac{1}{8}$ | $\frac{1}{8}$

$\frac{1}{5}$ ◯ $\frac{2}{8}$

5. $\frac{1}{6}$ | $\frac{1}{6}$ | $\frac{1}{6}$ | $\frac{1}{6}$

$\frac{1}{3}$ | $\frac{1}{3}$

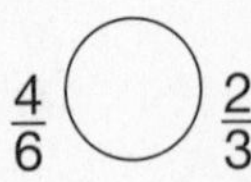

$\frac{4}{6}$ ◯ $\frac{2}{3}$

6. $\frac{1}{10}$ | $\frac{1}{10}$ | $\frac{1}{10}$

$\frac{1}{6}$

$\frac{3}{10}$ ◯ $\frac{1}{6}$

7. **Number Sense** Your body consists of $\frac{7}{10}$ water. Is more than $\frac{1}{2}$ your body water? Explain.

____

____

____

____

____

8. Two fractions have the same numerator, but different denominators. Is the fraction with the greater denominator greater than or less than the fraction with the lesser denominator?

____

____

____

____

9. **Draw a Picture** Draw a figure that is less than $\frac{1}{6}$.

10. Which fraction is greater than $\frac{1}{2}$?

A $\frac{1}{4}$

B $\frac{2}{6}$

C $\frac{3}{8}$

D $\frac{3}{4}$

Name ______________________

Fractions on the Number Line

1. Complete the number line by writing the missing fractions and mixed numbers.

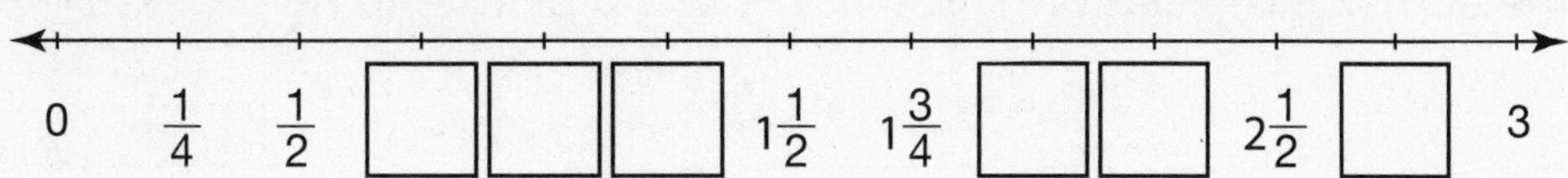

Compare. Write <, >, or =. Use the number line above to help.

2. $\frac{3}{4} \bigcirc \frac{1}{2}$

3. $1\frac{2}{4} \bigcirc 1\frac{1}{2}$

4. $1\frac{3}{4} \bigcirc 2\frac{1}{4}$

5. What is the order of $1\frac{1}{4}$, $2\frac{1}{2}$, and $1\frac{3}{4}$ from least to greatest?

____

Use the number line for **6** and **7**.

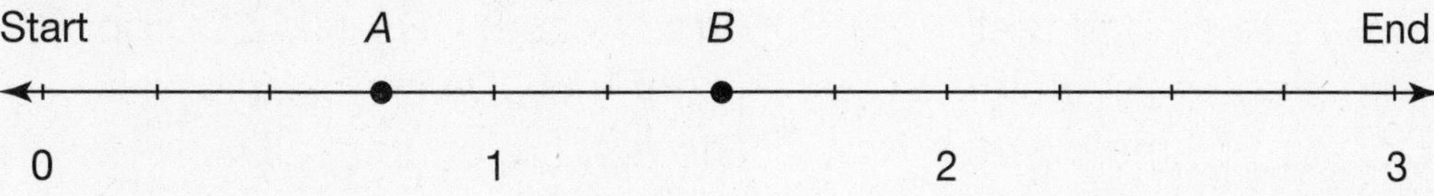

6. Lorne is running a 3-mile race. He stops at Water Stop A. How far did Lorne run?

____

7. How far is Water Stop B from the end of the race?

____

8. **Explain It** How can you compare two fractions by using a number line?

9. **Geometry** What fraction of the angles in this parallelogram are acute angles?

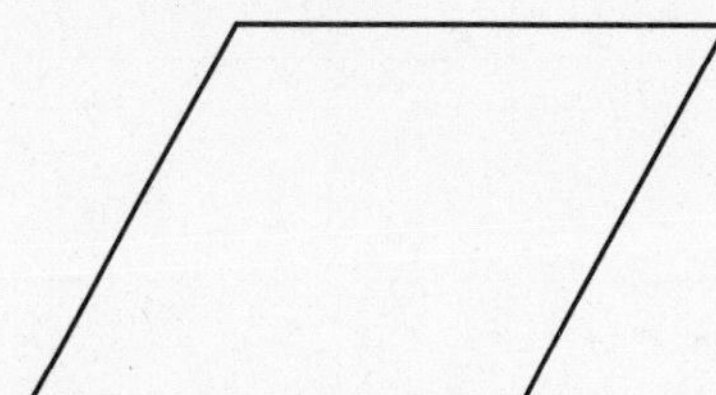

A $\frac{1}{4}$

B $\frac{1}{2}$

C $\frac{2}{3}$

D $\frac{3}{4}$

Name ______________________

Practice
12-8

Using Models to Add Fractions

Add. Write the sum in simplest form. You may draw a picture to help.

1. $\frac{3}{8} + \frac{4}{8}$

$\frac{1}{8}$	$\frac{1}{8}$	$\frac{1}{8}$

$\frac{1}{8}$	$\frac{1}{8}$	$\frac{1}{8}$	$\frac{1}{8}$

______

2. $\frac{2}{6} + \frac{2}{6}$

$\frac{1}{6}$	$\frac{1}{6}$

$\frac{1}{6}$	$\frac{1}{6}$

______

3. $\frac{3}{10} + \frac{4}{10}$ ______

4. $\frac{2}{4} + \frac{1}{4}$ ______

5. $\frac{1}{8} + \frac{5}{8}$ ______

6. $\frac{2}{5} + \frac{2}{5}$ ______

7. Marlon and Ricky ate a pizza that was divided into eighths. Marlon ate $\frac{2}{8}$ and Ricky ate $\frac{2}{8}$ of the pizza. How much of the pizza did they eat in all? Write your sum in simplest form.

______

8. Buddy has 8 CDs in his CD book. Six of the CDs are classic rock. The rest are country CDs. In simplest form, what fraction of the CDs are country CDs?

______

9. Write a Problem Write an addition problem that has $\frac{9}{10}$ as the sum.

______

______

______

______

10. Madison read $\frac{4}{10}$ of the chapters of a book Saturday and another $\frac{2}{10}$ Sunday. In simplest form, what fraction of the book did Madison read?

$\frac{1}{10}$	$\frac{1}{10}$	$\frac{1}{10}$	$\frac{1}{10}$

$\frac{1}{10}$	$\frac{1}{10}$

A $\frac{3}{4}$

B $\frac{3}{5}$

C $\frac{7}{10}$

D $\frac{1}{2}$

11. Of Tami's pets $\frac{2}{6}$ are dogs and $\frac{3}{6}$ are cats. What fraction of Tami's pets are dogs or cats?

______

Name ______________________

Practice
12-9

Using Models to Subtract Fractions

Subtract. Write the difference in simplest form. You may draw a picture to help.

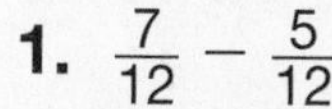

1. $\frac{7}{12} - \frac{5}{12}$

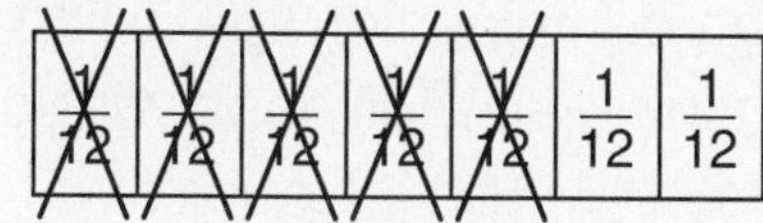

______

2. $\frac{5}{8} - \frac{2}{8}$

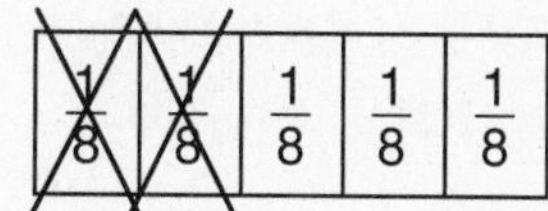

______

3. $\frac{9}{10} - \frac{4}{10}$ ______

4. $\frac{3}{6} - \frac{1}{6}$ ______

5. $\frac{7}{9} - \frac{4}{9}$ ______

6. $\frac{8}{10} - \frac{6}{10}$ ______

7. Patricia is responsible for washing $\frac{6}{8}$ of the desks in her classroom. She has already washed $\frac{4}{8}$ of the desks. What fraction of the desks does she still have to wash? Write your difference in simplest form. ______

8. **Write a Problem** Write a subtraction problem that has a difference of $\frac{1}{6}$.

______

9. Of the pets sold this week at a pet store, $\frac{5}{10}$ were dogs and $\frac{3}{10}$ were cats. What fraction describes how many more dogs were sold than cats? Write your difference in simplest form.

______

10. **Reasoning** Colin said that $\frac{7}{10} - \frac{2}{10} = \frac{5}{10}$. Louisa said that $\frac{7}{10} - \frac{2}{10} = \frac{1}{2}$. Who is correct?

______

______

11. Of the license plates that Sue saw, $\frac{5}{8}$ were from California and $\frac{1}{8}$ were from Oregon. In simplest form, what fraction of the plates were from other states?

______

12. What is $\frac{8}{9} - \frac{4}{9}$?

A $\frac{2}{3}$

B $\frac{4}{9}$

C $\frac{5}{9}$

D $\frac{1}{3}$

Name ______________________________

Practice
12-10

Problem Solving: Make a Table and Look for a Pattern

Complete each table to solve.

1. Roses at a flower shop are sold in packages of 12. Each package contains 4 red roses. How many red roses will you get if you buy 60 roses?

Red Roses	4				
Total Roses	12				

2. There are 20 lollipops in each package of Yum's Lollipops. Each package contains 4 grape lollipops. How many grape lollipops will you get if you buy 100 lollipops?

Grape Lollipops	4				
Total Lollipops	20				

3. There are 9 bottles of salsa in a gift pack of Pedro's Salsa. In each gift pack, 2 of the bottles are extra spicy. Suppose someone buys 45 bottles. How many of the bottles will be extra spicy?

Extra Spicy Bottles	2				
Total Bottles	9				

4. Reasoning Look back at Exercise 3. Suppose Jackie bought 27 bottles.

a. How many of the bottles would not be extra spicy?

____

b. How many more bottles are not extra spicy than are extra spicy?

____

5. In a package of 25 colored pencils, 8 are red. If you bought 125 pencils, how many would be red?

Red Pencils	8				
Total Pencils	25				

6. Write a Problem Write a problem that can be solved by making a table and using a pattern. Then solve the problem.

____

____

____

Name ______________________________

Practice
13-1

Fractions and Decimals

Write a fraction and a decimal for each shaded part.

1. 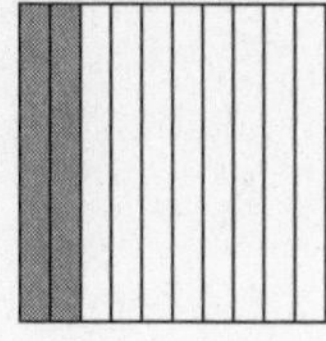

____

2. 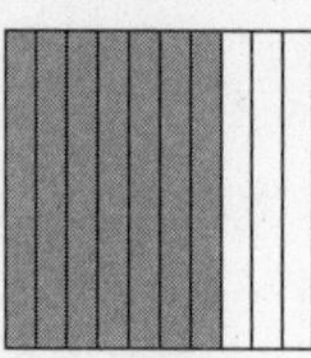

____

3. 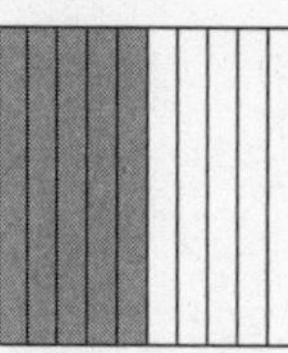

____

4. 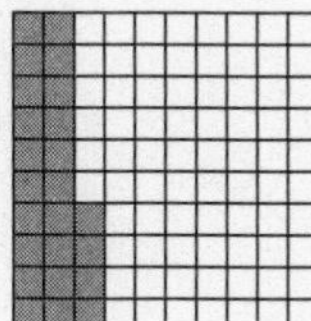

____

5. 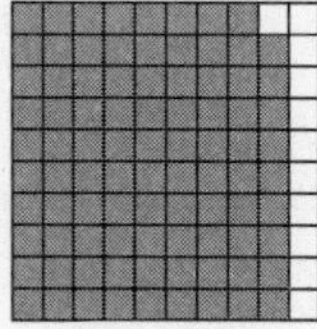

____

6. 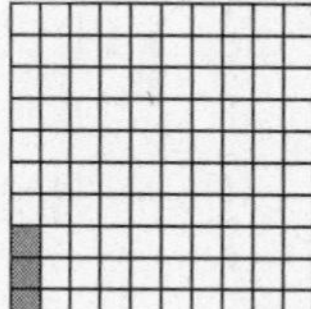

____

7. **Number Sense** Len bought a pizza that was cut into 10 slices. He ate 4 of the slices. What decimal represents the part of the pizza that remains?

____

8. There are 100 players in the soccer league. Of those players, 15 are on the Sharks. Write a fraction and a decimal to show what part of the league's players are on the Sharks.

____

9. What fraction is equal to 0.8?

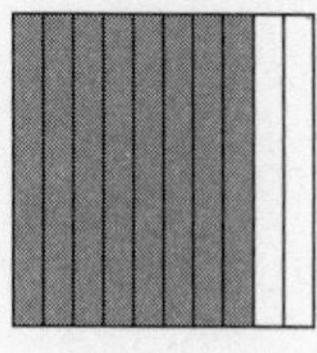

____

10. Which decimal is equivalent to $\frac{30}{100}$?

A 30.0

B 3.0

C 0.3

D 0.03

Name ______________________

Practice
13-2

Using Money to Understand Decimals

Complete.

1. $5.38 = ☐ dollars + ☐ dimes + ☐ pennies

   5.38 = ☐ ones + ☐ tenths + ☐ hundredths

2. $9.15 = ☐ dollars + ☐ dimes + ☐ pennies

   9.15 = ☐ ones + ☐ tenths + ☐ hundredths

3. $6.09 = ☐ dollars + ☐ dimes + ☐ pennies

   6.09 = ☐ ones + ☐ tenths + ☐ hundredths

4. $3.82 = ☐ dollars + ☐ dimes + ☐ pennies

   3.82 = ☐ ones + ☐ tenths + ☐ hundredths

Write each number with a decimal point.

5. eight and twenty-six hundredths

   ____

6. seven and nine hundredths

   ____

7. two and thirty hundredths

   ____

8. four and nineteen hundredths

   ____

9. **Draw a Picture** Using rectangles for dollars and circles for coins, make a drawing to represent $2.65.

10. Which money amount represents 3 dollars, 4 quarters, 2 dimes, 3 nickels?

    A $3.95

    B $4.10

    C $4.25

    D $4.35

Name ______________________

Practice
13-3

Adding and Subtracting Money

Find each sum or difference.

1. $7.29 − 1.03

2. $3.50 + 2.91

3. $6.00 − 2.59

4. $17.99 − 13.86

5. $20.00 − 18.42

6. $12.04 + 3.16

7. $4.21 + 3.99

8. $6.18 − 3.19

9. $7.83 + $0.62 ________

10. $16.02 − $5.19 ________

11. $18.21 + $14.36 ________

12. $27.36 − $15.29 ________

13. $1.25 + $0.59 + $3.57 ________

14. $30.00 − $21.78 ________

15. Cindy bought a T-shirt for $17.59 and a baseball cap for $12.85. How much money did Cindy spend altogether?

____

16. Terrell bought a book for $15.97. He paid for the book with a $20 bill. How much change should Terrell receive back?

____

17. **Explain It** How is adding and subtracting with money like adding and subtracting whole numbers?

____

____

____

____

____

18. Sam paid for a notebook that costs $2.76 with a $10 bill. What was his change?

A $7.24

B $7.34

C $8.24

D $12.76

Name ______________________________

Practice
13-4

Problem Solving: Draw a Picture and Write a Number Sentence

Solve. Draw a picture and write a number sentence.

1. Candi and Randy each have a CD with the same number of songs. On Candi's CD, $\frac{5}{8}$ of the songs are ballads. On Randy's CD, $\frac{2}{8}$ of the songs are ballads. How much more of Candi's CD contains ballads than Randy's CD?

____

2. Jaime is painting his backyard fence. He paints $\frac{4}{10}$ of the slats red. Then he paints $\frac{2}{10}$ of the slats blue. In simplest form, what fraction of the fence did Jaime paint in all?

____

3. Troy completed $\frac{5}{12}$ of his book report before dinner. He completed another $\frac{3}{12}$ of the report after dinner. In simplest form, how much of the report did he finish in all?

____

4. Sandra has read $\frac{3}{4}$ of a comic book. Tricia has read $\frac{1}{4}$ of the same comic book. How much more of the comic book has Sandra read than Tricia?

____

5. **Write a Problem** Write a real-world problem with fractions that you can solve by drawing a picture and writing a number sentence.

____

____

____

____

____

6. **Reasoning** When you add or subtract fractions with the same denominator, what happens to the denominator in your answer?

____

____

____

Name ____________________

Practice
13-5

Problem Solving: Missing or Extra Information

For **1** and **2**, decide if the problem has extra or missing information. Solve if you have enough information.

1. Each time Kendra walks Mr. Karl's dog, he gives her $3. Kendra walks the dog for 30 minutes. If she walks the dog on Monday, Tuesday, and Thursday, how much money does Kendra make each week for walking Mr. Karl's dog?

2. Dylan trades baseball cards with his friends. He received all of his cards as a gift from his grandmother. If Dylan trades 58 baseball cards away and gets 62 back, how many cards does he have now?

3. Write a Problem Write a problem about Marie who has to do homework in math, reading, and social studies. Include extra information in your problem. Then solve it.

4. Tommy has 36 CDs and 24 DVDs. All of his CDs are either rock and roll or hip hop. He has 15 drama DVDs and 6 comedy DVDs. What information do you need to find how many hip hop CDs Tommy has?

A the number of rock and roll CDs

B the number of music DVDs

C the number of rap CDs

D the number of country CDs

Name ______________________

Practice
14-1

Understanding Measurement

Estimate each length. Then measure to the nearest inch.

1.

____

2.

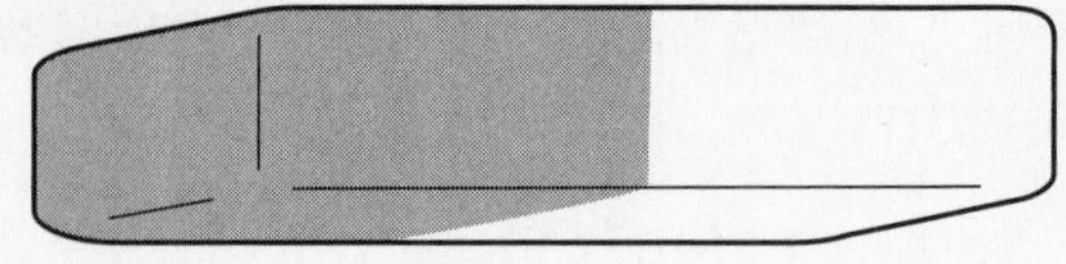

____

3.

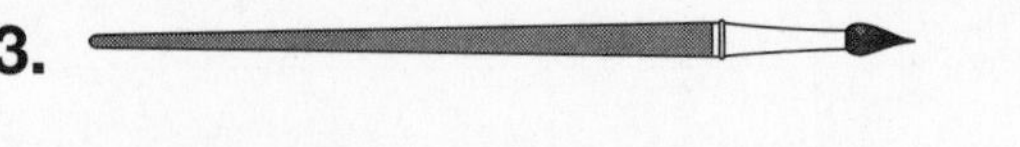

____

4.

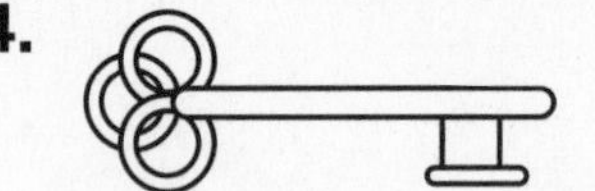

____

5. Reasoning To measure the length of a closet, Aaron used his foot and measured 6 foot-lengths. His father measured 4 foot-lengths. Could they be measuring the same closet? Explain.

____

____

6. Draw a line segment that is 2 inches long.

7. Writing to Explain Describe how to use a ruler to measure to the nearest inch.

____

____

8. Which paper clip is 1 inch long?

A

B

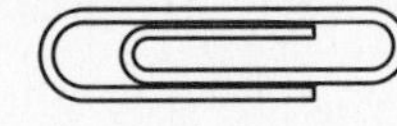

C

D

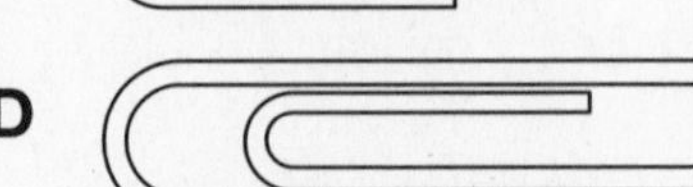

Name ______________________

Practice 14-2

Fractions of an Inch

Measure the length of each object to the nearest $\frac{1}{2}$ inch and $\frac{1}{4}$ inch.

1. 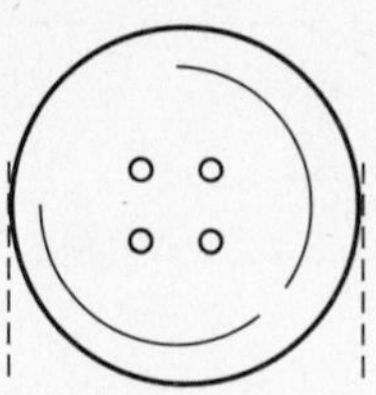

____

2. 

____

3. 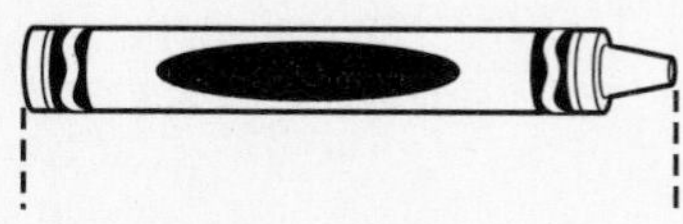

____

4. 

____

5. Draw a line segment that is $1\frac{1}{2}$ inches long.

6. **Geometry** Draw a square with sides that are each 1 inch long.

7. **Reasoning** Eric and Madison both measured the same trading card. Eric says the card is about 3 inches long. Madison says it is about $2\frac{3}{4}$ inches long. Their teacher says they are both correct. How is that possible?

____

____

____

8. Which can **NOT** be a length measured to the nearest $\frac{1}{4}$ inch?

A $\frac{1}{4}$ inch **B** $\frac{3}{8}$ inch 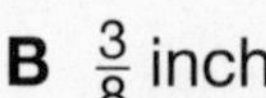 **C** $\frac{1}{2}$ inch 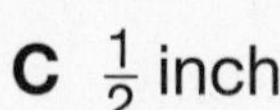 **D** $\frac{3}{4}$ inch

Name ______________________

Practice
14-3

Using Inches, Feet, Yards, and Miles

In **1** through **8**, change the units.

1. 3 feet, 3 inches
1 foot = 12 inches
3 × 12 inches = 36 inches
36 inches + ☐ inches =
☐ inches

2. 2 yards, 1 foot
1 yard = 3 feet
2 × 3 feet = ☐ feet
☐ + 1 foot = ☐ feet

3. How many inches are in 2 yards?

______

4. How many feet are in 5 yards?

______

5. 2 feet 7 inches = ☐ inches

6. 5 feet 6 inches = ☐ inches

7. 4 feet 8 inches = ☐ inches

8. 3 yards 2 feet = ☐ feet

In **9** and **10**, choose the better estimate.

9. The depth of a swimming pool
10 feet or 10 miles

____

10. The length of your desk
2 inches or 2 feet

____

11. **Explain It** How do you convert feet to inches?

____

____

12. **Reasonableness** Would you measure the length between two cities in feet or miles?

____

____

13. Which measure is equal to 3 feet 7 inches?

A 37 inches **B** 43 inches **C** 44 inches **D** 55 inches

14. Which unit would be best to measure the length of your pinkie finger?

A Inches **B** Feet **C** Yards **D** Miles

Name ______________________

Practice
14-4

Customary Units of Capacity

Choose the better estimate for each.

1. 
1 c or 1 gal
______

2. 
3 qt or 3 gal
______

3. 
1 pt or 1 gal
______

4. 
10 qt or 10 gal
______

5. coffee pot
1 c or 1 gal
______

6. bowl of soup
1 pt or 1 gal
______

7. thermos
1 qt or 1 gal
______

8. small milk carton
1 c or 1 gal
______

Choose the better unit to measure the capacity of each.

9. hot tub
qt or gal
______

10. shampoo bottle
pt or gal
______

11. bucket
c or gal
______

12. sports cooler
qt or gal
______

13. **Reasonableness** John has 4 cups filled with fruit juice. He said that he has a gallon of fruit juice. Is his statement reasonable? Explain why or why not.

____

____

____

14. **Estimation** Which measurement best describes the capacity of a kitchen sink?

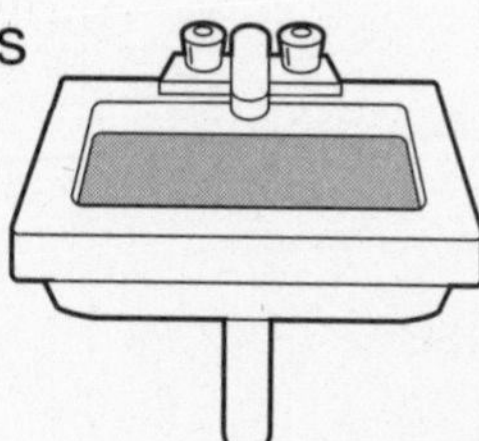

A 5 quarts **B** 5 pints **C** 5 cups **D** 5 gallons

Name ________________________

Units of Weight

Choose the better estimate for each.

1. 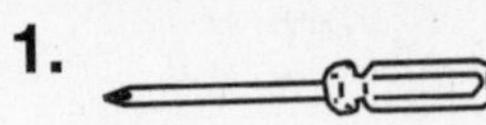
3 oz or 3 lb
____

2. 
30 oz or 30 lb
____

3. 
2 oz or 2 lb
____

4. 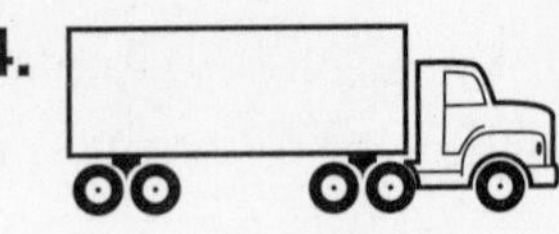
500 lb or 5 T
____

5. DVD
1 oz or 1 lb
____

6. chair
20 oz or 20 lb
____

7. cell phone
6 oz or 6 lb
____

8. computer
10 oz or 10 lb
____

Choose the better unit to measure the weight of each.

9. car
lb or T
____

10. strawberry
oz or lb
____

11. baseball
oz or lb
____

12. book
lb or T
____

13. **Explain It** Emily said the larger an object is, the more it weighs. Is Emily correct? Explain why or why not.

____

____

____

14. **Estimation** Which of the following objects can best be measured in ounces?

A pencil　　**B** couch　　**C** desk　　**D** doghouse

Name ___________________________

Problem Solving: Act It Out and Use Reasoning

1. Use grid paper. Draw the front, side, and top views of the figure shown below.

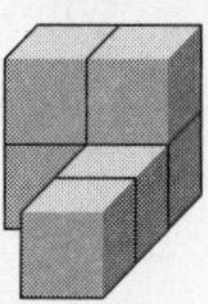

Front Right Side Top

2. Use grid paper. Draw the front, side, and top views of the figure shown below.

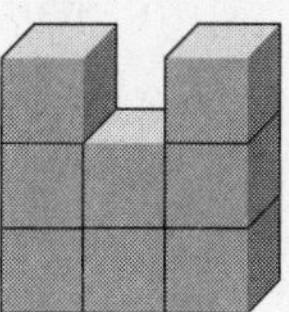

Front Right Side Top

3. Use cubes to build the figure shown in these pictures.

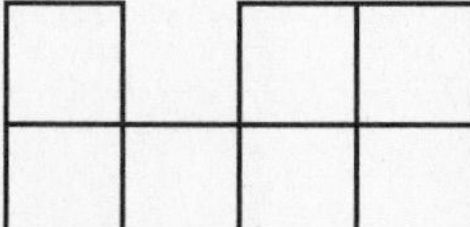 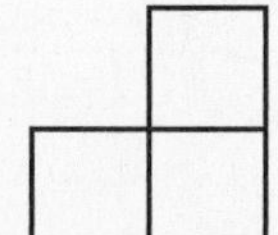 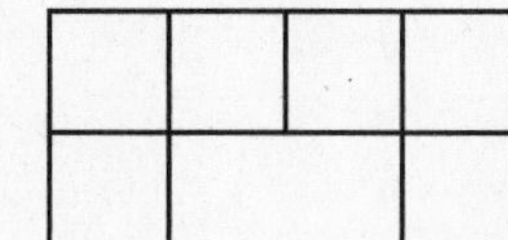

Front Right Side Top

4. **Reasoning** If the front, side, and top views are all the same, what type of figure are you looking at? Explain.

____

____

____

Name ______________________

Practice
15-1

Using Centimeters and Decimeters

In **1** through **4**, estimate each length. Then measure to the nearest centimeter.

1. 

____

2. 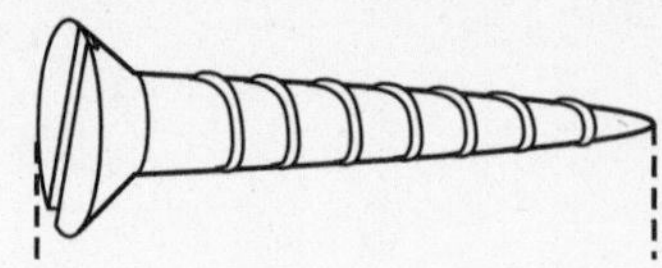

____

3. 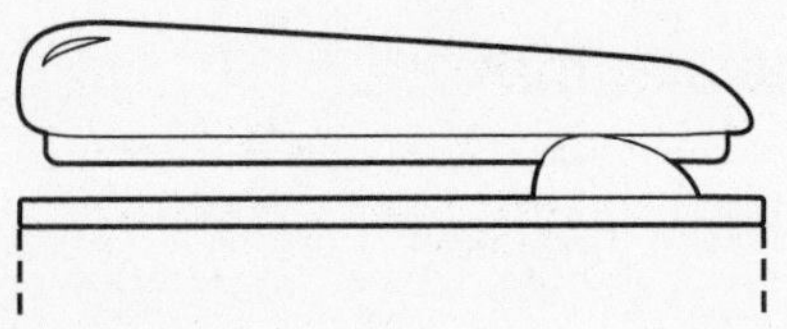

____

4. 

____

5. Draw a Diagram Draw a line segment that is 6 centimeters long.

6. Estimation Estimate the length of your desk in centimeters. Then measure the length of your desk.

____

7. Reasonableness Marian measured the length of a piece of paper as 7 decimeters. George measured the same length as 70 centimeters. Their teacher said they both are correct. Is that possible?

____

____

____

8. What is the length of the box of tape to the nearest centimeter?

A 2 centimeters **C** 4 centimeters

B 3 centimeters **D** 5 centimeters

Name ______________________

Practice
15-2

Using Meters and Kilometers

In **1** and **2**, convert the units. Complete.

1. How many centimeters are there in 3 meters 25 centimeters?

____

2. 5 meters = ■ centimeters

____

In **3** and **4**, choose the better estimate.

3. The length of a key
3 centimeters or 3 meters

____

4. The length of bike path
2 meters or 2 kilometers

____

5. Complete the table.

km	1	2	3	4
m	1,000	2,000		

6. **Estimation** Is the length of a pencil greater than or less than 1 meter? Explain.

____

____

____

7. **Reasonableness** Andy lives 6 kilometers from the mall. He said he lives 600 meters away from the mall. Is Andy's statement reasonable? Explain.

____

____

____

8. Which is the best estimate for the length of a calculator?

A 1 meter **B** 1 centimeter **C** 10 meters **D** 10 centimeters

Name ______________________

Practice
15-3

Metric Units of Capacity

Choose the better estimate for each.

1. 

2 mL or 2 L

______

2. 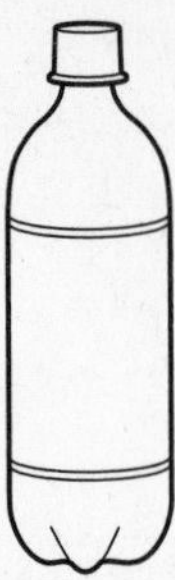

2 mL or 2 L

______

3. 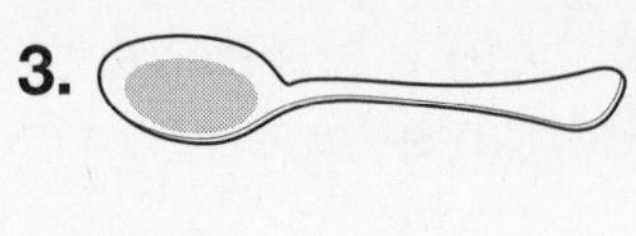

5 mL or 5 L

______

4. 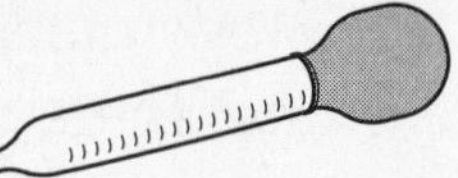

1 mL or 1 L

______

5. kitchen sink
2 L or 20 L

______

6. coffee cup
250 mL or 25 L

______

7. thermos
2 L or 20 L

______

8. pitcher
40 mL or 4 L

______

Choose the better unit to measure the capacity of each.

9. tea cup
mL or L

______

10. bath tub
mL or L

______

11. glass of juice
mL or L

______

12. washing machine
mL or L

______

13. **Reasoning** A liter is equal to 100 centiliters. Is a centiliter a greater measure than a milliliter? Explain.

____

____

____

14. **Estimation** Which is the best estimate for the capacity of a large bottle of water?

A 1 L 

C 4 L

B 400 mL

D 40 mL

Name ______________________________

Units of Mass

Choose the better estimate for each.

1. 

3 g or 3 kg

______

2. 

40 g or 40 kg

______

3. 

250 g or 25 kg

______

4. 

30 g or 300 g

______

5. crayon
20 g or 200 g

______

6. large dog
5 kg or 50 kg

______

7. quarter
5 g or 500 g

______

8. adult male
7 kg or 70 kg

______

Choose the best tool to measure each.

9. the mass of a phone ______

10. the length of a crayon ______

11. the temperature ______

12. the time for dinner ______

13. the capacity of a bowl ______

a. 

b. 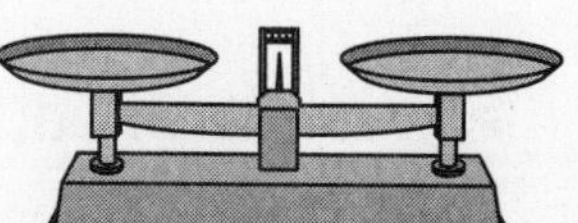

c. 

d. 

e. 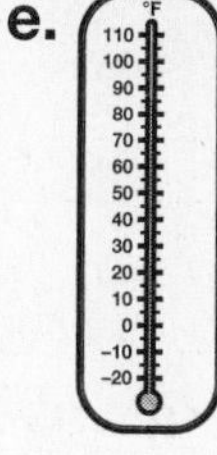

14. Writing to Explain Would you use grams or kilograms to find the mass of a letter? Explain.

____

____

____

15. Estimation Which is the best estimate for the mass of a pair of sneakers?

A 1 kg **B** 1 g **C** 10 kg **D** 10 g

Name ______________________________

Practice
15-5

Problem Solving: Make a Table and Look for a Pattern

Complete the table. Explain the pattern.

1. Fred is putting tables together to make one long table. Each table is shaped like a square and is 3 meters long. What is the length of 4 tables? 5 tables?

Number of Tables	1	2	3	4	5
Total Length	3 m	6 m	9 m		

____

____

____

____

2. Sheila is cutting a board that is 72 centimeters long. She is cutting the board into pieces that are each 9 centimeters long. What is the length of the board after Sheila has made 3 cuts? 4 cuts?

Number of Pieces	0	1	2	3	4
Length of Board Left	72 cm	63 cm	54 cm		

____

____

____

____

3. Cindy is linking toy train cars together. What is the total length of the train with 4 cars? 5 cars?

Number of Train Cars	1	2	3	4	5
Total Length	20 cm	40 cm	60 cm		

____

____

____

____

4. Dennis is stacking boxes on top of each other. Each box is 8 centimeters high. What is the height of 4 boxes? 5 boxes?

Number of Boxes	1	2	3	4	5
Total Height	8 cm	16 cm	24 cm		

____

____

____

____

Name ____________________

Understanding Perimeter

Find the perimeter of each polygon.

1. 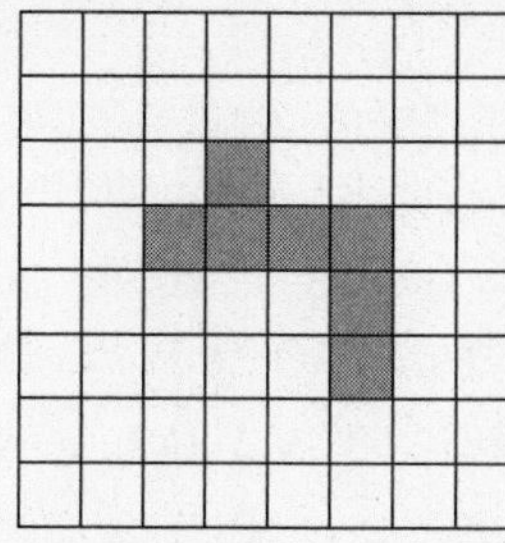

2. 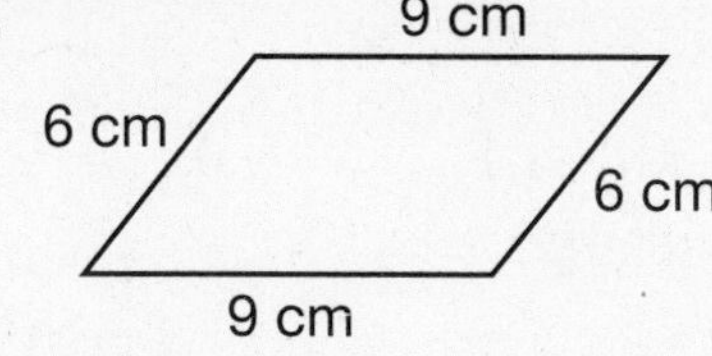

3. 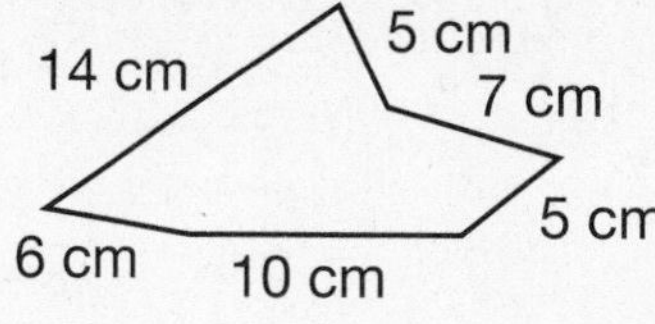

____________________ ____________________ ____________________

Draw a figure with the given perimeter.

4. 10 units

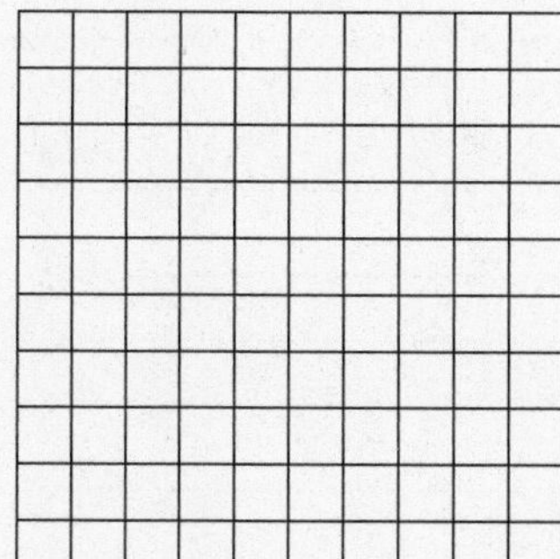

5. 22 units

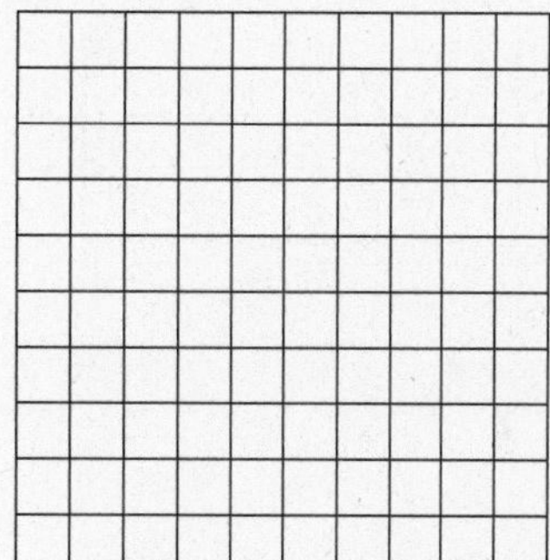

6. A park has the shape of a trapezoid. Two of the sides are 25 meters long. The other two sides are 40 meters and 20 meters long. What is the perimeter of the park?

____

7. Mr. Anders wants to put a fence around his backyard. His backyard is rectangular. The lengths of the sides are 75 yards, 45 yards, 75 yards, and 45 yards. How much fencing will Mr. Anders need?

____

8. **Explain It** When finding the perimeter of a figure on a grid, why do you not count the spaces inside the grid?

____

____

9. Which rectangle has a perimeter of 16 units?

A Length 5 units, width 3 units

B Length 10 units, width 6 units

C Length 8 units, width 1 unit

D Length 6 units, width 3 units

Name ______________________

Perimeter of Common Shapes

Use a centimeter ruler to measure the length of the sides of each polygon. Find each perimeter.

1.

____

2.

____

Find the perimeter of each figure.

3.

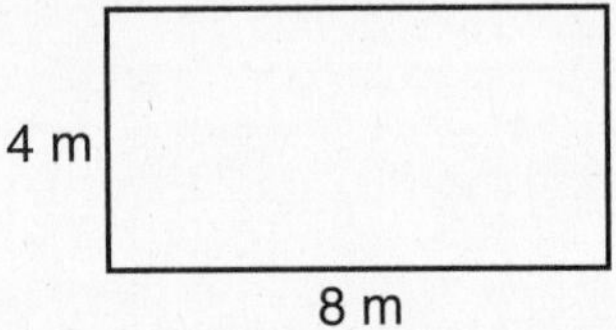

____

4.

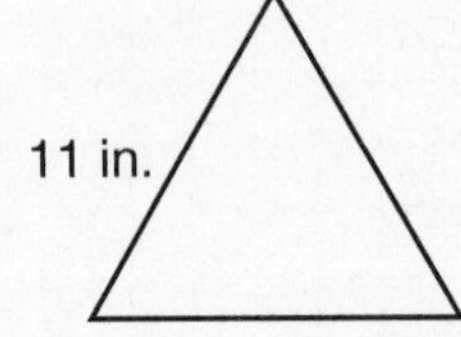

____

5. The largest bedroom in Lauren's house is shaped like a square with sides of 6 yards. What is the perimeter of that bedroom?

____

6. The basketball court at Johnson Elementary School is in the shape of a rectangle. It is 92 feet long and 46 feet wide. What is the perimeter of the basketball court?

____

7. Reasonableness A square and a pentagon each have 9-inch sides. Are their perimeters the same? Explain your answer.

____

____

8. What is the perimeter of a hexagon that has sides of 12 inches?

A 60 inches **B** 66 inches **C** 72 inches **D** 84 inches

Name ______________________________

Different Shapes with the Same Perimeter

Draw a figure with the given perimeter on the grid paper.

1. 10 units

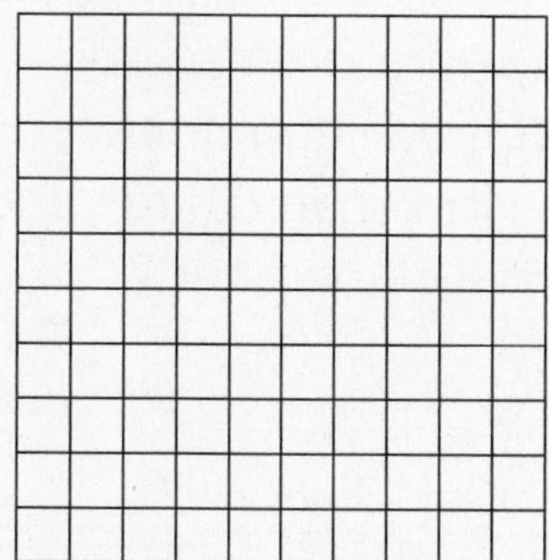

2. 16 units

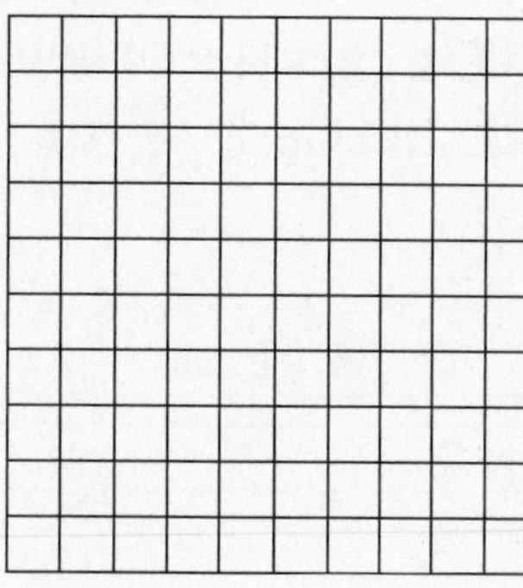

3. 14 units

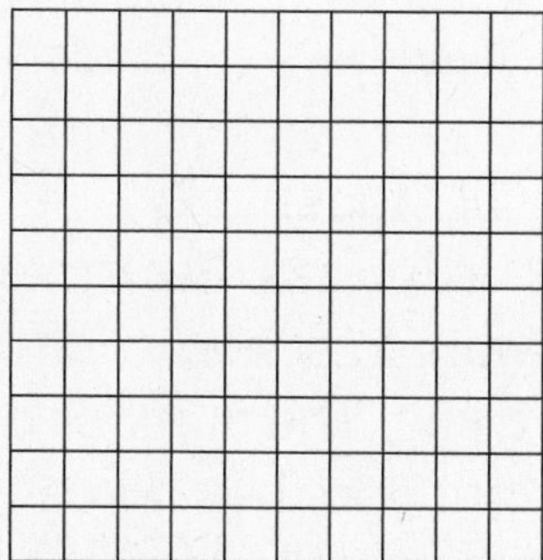

4. 18 units

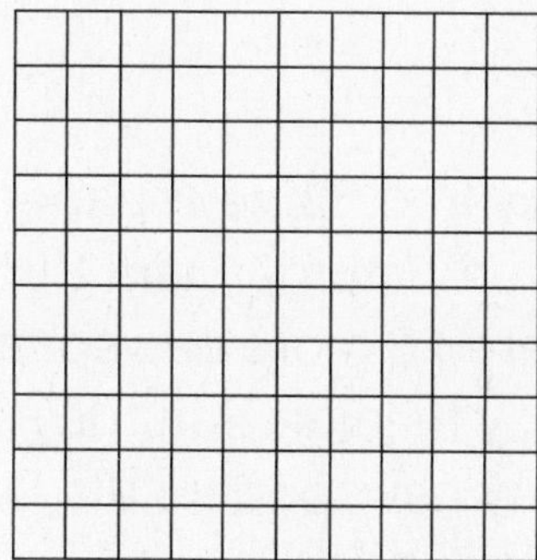

5. Writing to Explain Can you draw a square with a perimeter of 20 units? Explain why or why not.

____

____

____

6. Number Sense Name the lengths of the sides of three rectangles with a perimeter of 12 units. Use only whole numbers.

____

____

____

7. Which figures have the same perimeter?

A

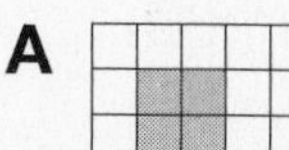

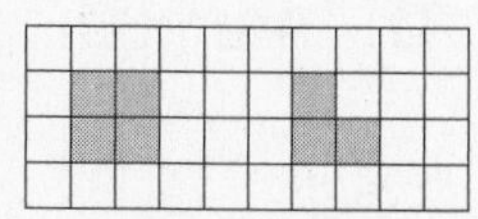

C

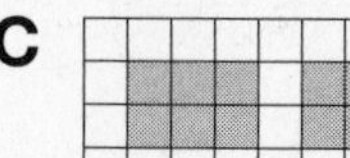

B

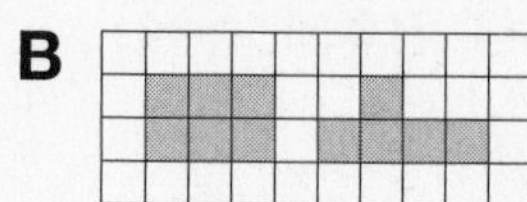

D

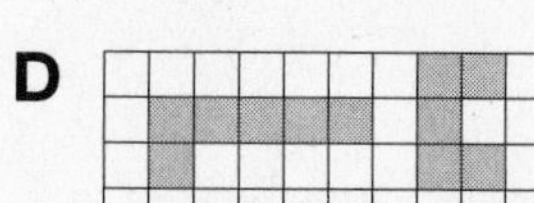

Name ______________________

Practice **16-4**

Problem Solving: Try, Check, and Revise

1. Carly and Rob combined their DVD collection. Now they have 42 DVDs altogether. Carly had 4 more DVDs than Rob. How many DVDs did Carly have?

____

2. There are 33 students in the band. There are 6 more fifth-grade students than third-grade students. There is an equal number of third- and fourth-grade students. How many third-grade students are in the band?

____

33 students in all

3rd:?	4th:?	5th:?
Same as Grade 4	Same as Grade 3	6 more than Grade 3

3. Dave delivered 52 newspapers all together on Saturday and Sunday. He delivered 8 more newspapers on Sunday than on Saturday. How many newspapers did Dave deliver on Sunday?

____

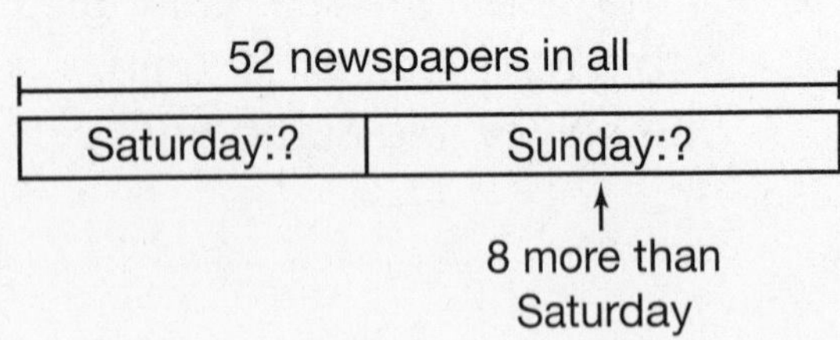

4. There are 24 students in Ms. Messing's class. Six more students walk to school than ride their bikes. The number of students that ride their bikes is the same as the number of students that are driven to school. How many students walk to school?

____

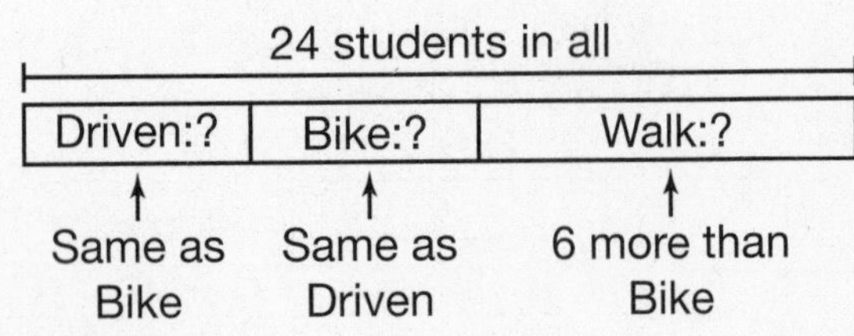

5. Jill is thinking of two numbers. They have a sum of 16 and a difference of 6. What are the two numbers?

A 16 and 6 **B** 13 and 3 **C** 12 and 4 **D** 11 and 5

Name ______________________

Understanding Area

Find the area of each figure.

1. 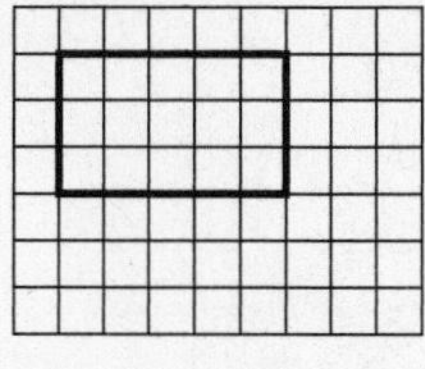

□ = 1 square cm

____

2. 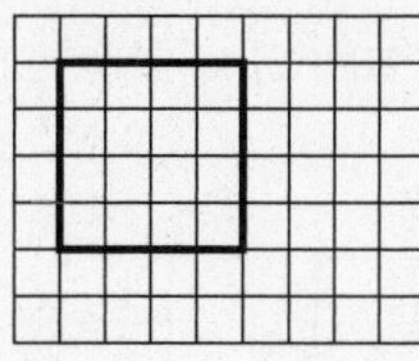

□ = 1 square in.

____

3. 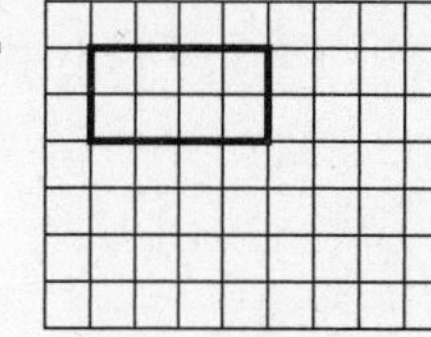

□ = 1 square m

____

4. 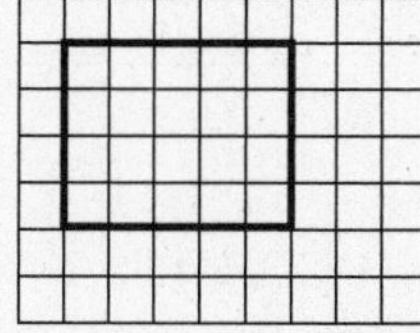

□ = 1 square ft

____

5. 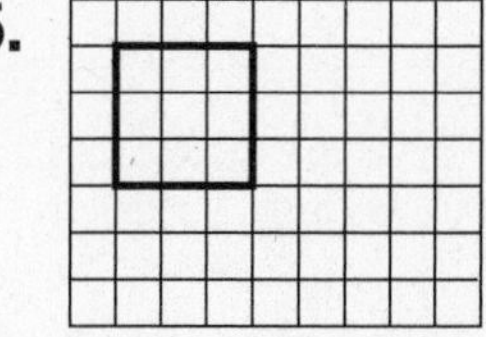

□ = 1 square cm

____

6. 6 in.

12 in.

____

7. **Draw a Picture** On the grid, draw as many different rectangles as you can with areas of 12 square units.

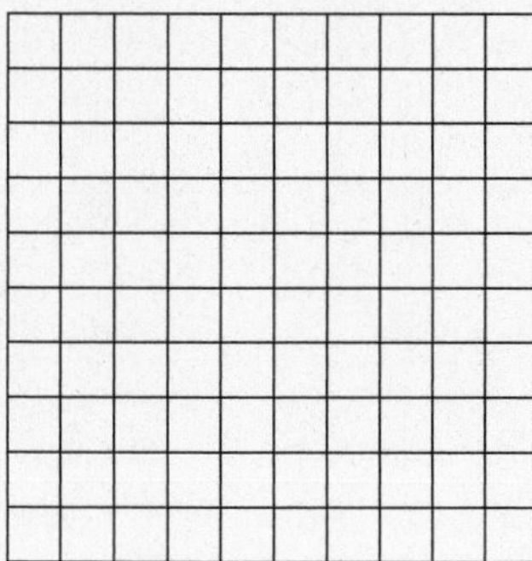

8. **Reasoning** Rectangular doghouses come in two sizes at the Super Z. The smaller size is 2 feet by 1 feet. The larger size is 4 feet by 2 feet. How many square feet greater is the larger doghouse?

____

9. What is the area of a square with sides of 5 inches?

A 10 square inches

B 20 square inches

C 25 square inches

D 50 square inches

Name ______________________

Practice **16-6**

Estimating and Measuring Area

Find the area of each figure in square units.

1. 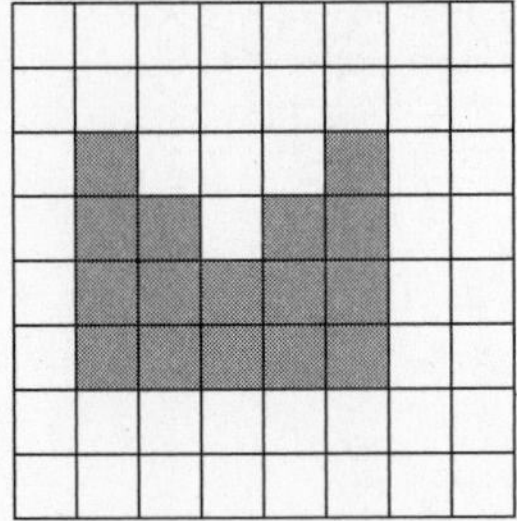

____

2. 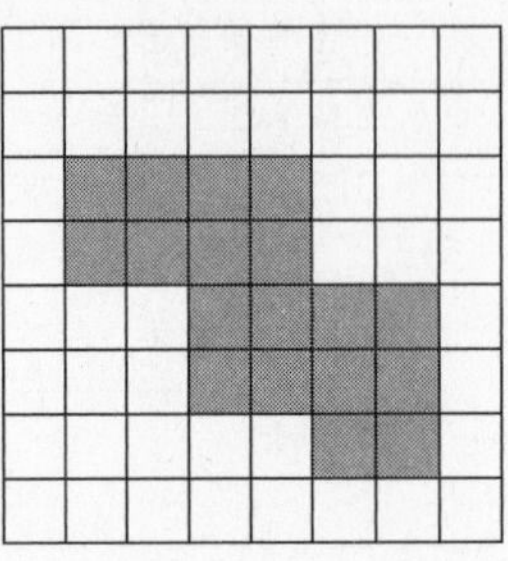

____

3. 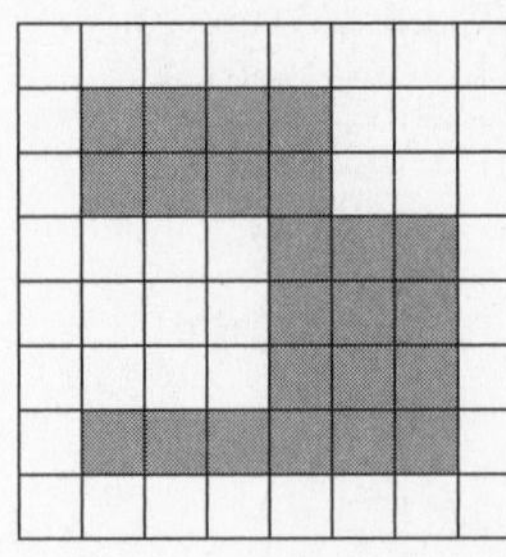

____

4. 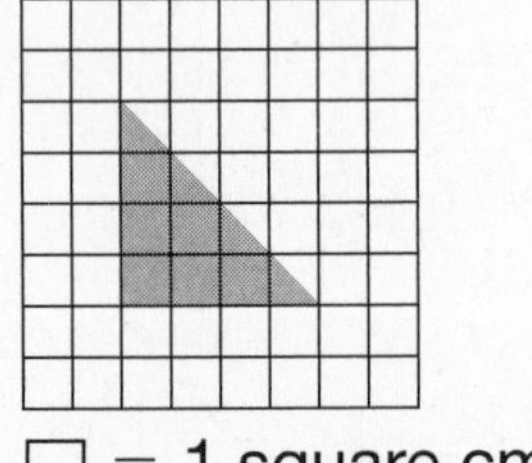

☐ = 1 square cm

____

5. 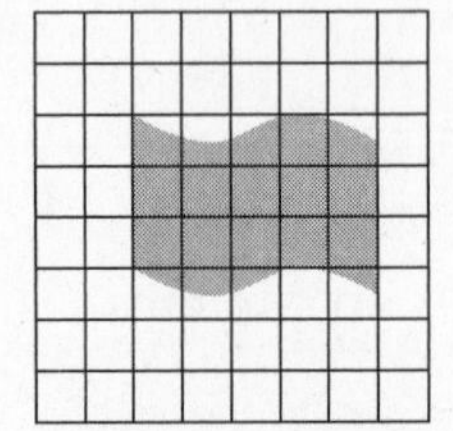

☐ = 1 square foot

____

6. 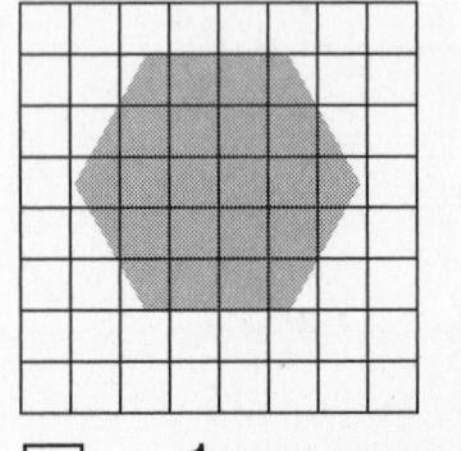

☐ = 1 square inch

____

7. Reasoning Use the grid. Draw two different figures that each have a perimeter of 14 units. Then find the area of each.

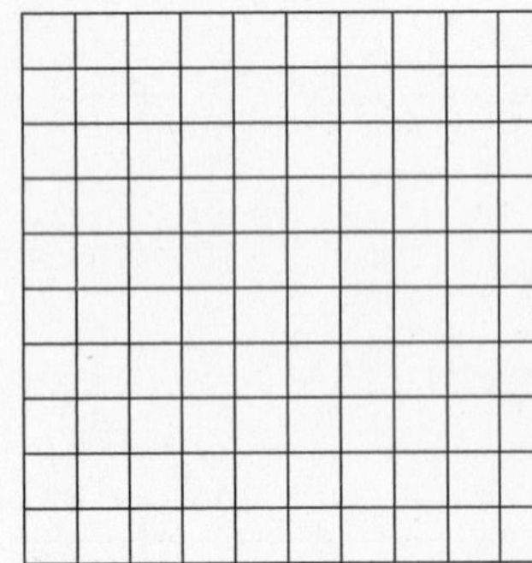

8. Explain It What is the difference between the perimeter and the area of a polygon?

____

____

____

____

9. What is the area of the figure to the right?

A 24 square units

B 25 square units

C 26 square units

D 27 square units

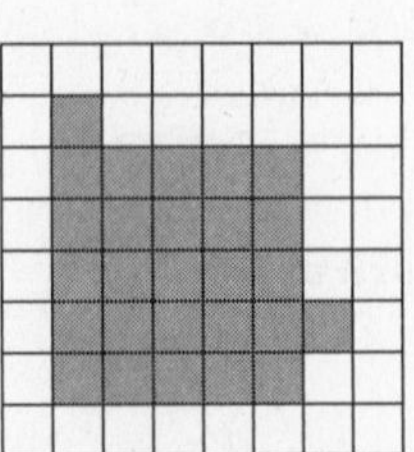

Name ______________________

Volume

Find the volume of each figure in cubic units.

1. 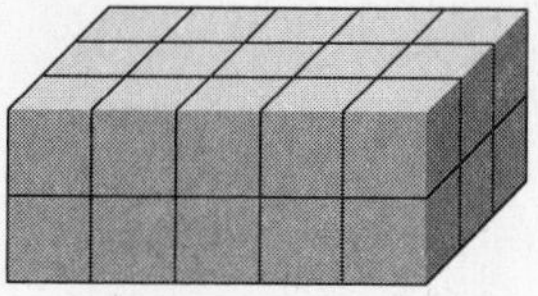
____

2. 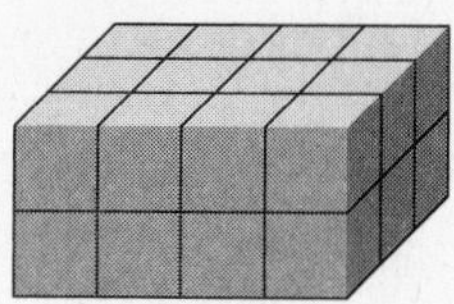
____

3. 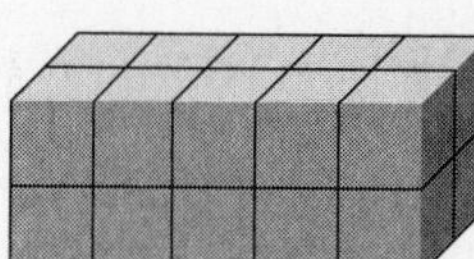
____

4. 
____

5. 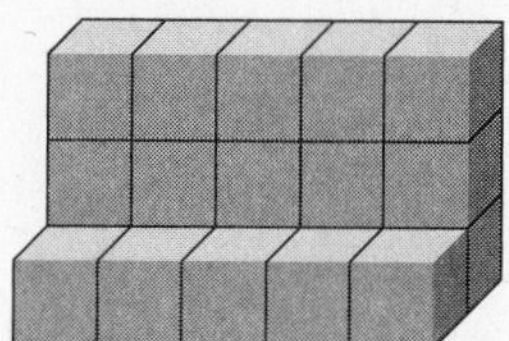
____

6. 
____

7. **Estimation** Use the cubes shown at the right to estimate the volume of the rectangular prism.

____

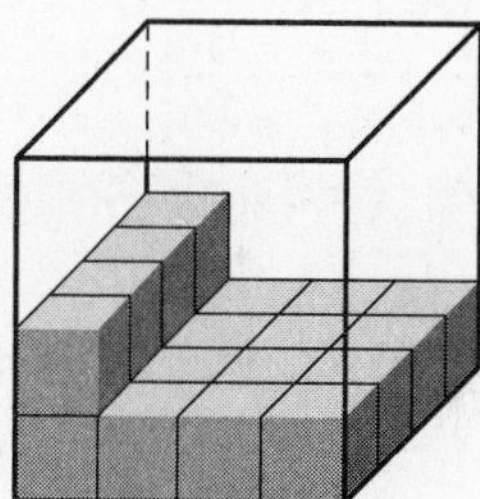

8. Kevin made a rectangular prism with 8 cubes in each layer. The prism has 4 layers. What is the volume of the rectangular prism?

____

9. **Explain It** How is finding volume different from finding area?

____

____

____

10. What is the volume of the figure at the right?

A 12 cubic units **C** 27 cubic units

B 24 cubic units **D** 36 cubic units

Name ______________________

Practice 16-8

Problem Solving: Solve a Simpler Problem

Solve. Use simpler problems.

1. Ms. Finn is going to tile her kitchen floor. The shaded part of the figure is the part that needs to be tiled. What is the area of the shaded part?

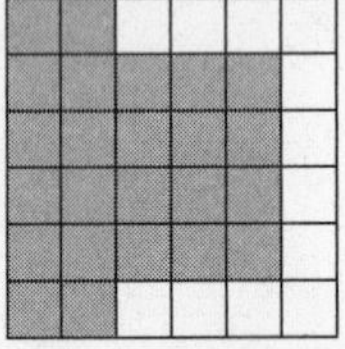

□ = 1 square yard

____

2. Alice is going to paint one of the walls in her bedroom. The shaded part of the figure is the part that needs to be painted. What is the area of the shaded part?

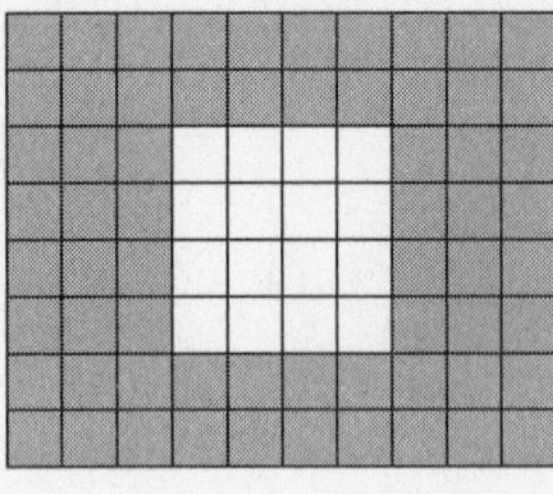

□ = 1 square foot

____

3. Harrison High School has an H painted on the football field. The shaded part of the figure is the part that needs to be painted. What is the area of the shaded part?

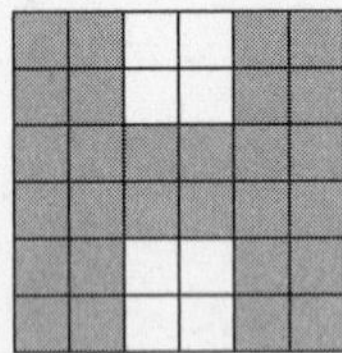

□ = 1 square meter

____

4. Mr. Rosen is going to repair the tiles in a shower. The shaded part of the figure is the part that needs to be tiled. What is the area of the shaded part?

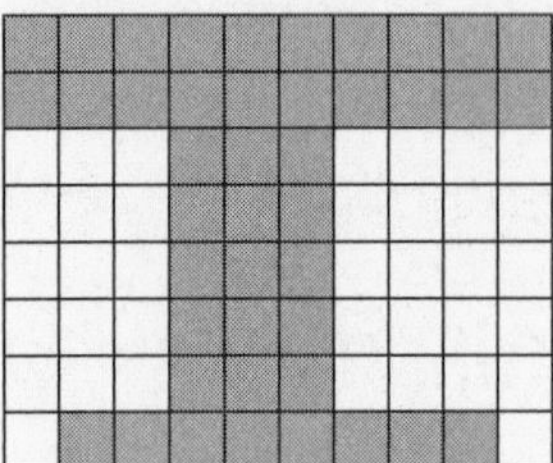

□ = 1 square foot

____

5. Luann is going to paint an L on her fence. The shaded part of the figure is the part that needs to be painted. What is the area of the shaded part?

____

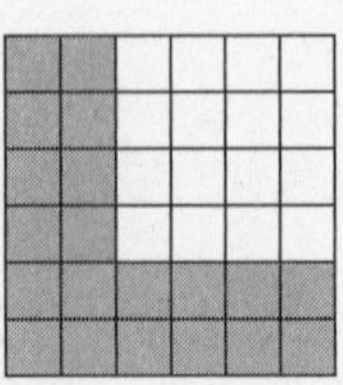

□ = 1 square inch

Name ____________________

Time to the Half Hour and Quarter Hour

Write the time shown on each clock in two ways.

1. 

____

____

2. 

____

____

3. 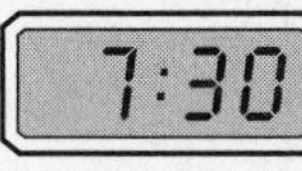

____

____

4. 

____

____

5. 

____

____

6. 

____

____

7. **Reasoning** The school bus stops at Randy's stop at 8:15 A.M. Randy arrived at the bus stop at quarter after 8. Did he miss the bus? Explain.

____

____

____

8. Which does **NOT** describe the time shown on the clock?

A five forty-five

B five fifteen

C quarter after five

D fifteen minutes after five

Name ____________________

Time to the Minute

Write the time shown on each clock in two ways.

1. 

____

____

2. 

____

____

3. 

____

____

4. 

____

____

5. 

____

____

6. 

____

____

7. **Geometry** What type of angle is formed by a clock's hands when it is 3:00? ______________

8. The movie Mike watched lasted 1 hour 26 minutes. How many minutes did the movie last? ______________

9. Jan's alarm clock sounded at the time shown on the clock below. At what time did the alarm clock sound?

A six ten

B six twenty-two

C six thirty-eight

D seven twenty-two

Name ________________________

Units of Time

Change the units. Complete.

1. 5 hours = ■■■ minutes

____

2. 3 weeks = ■■ days

____

3. 8 weeks = ■■ days

____

4. 6 hours = ■■■ minutes

____

5. How many minutes are in 3 hours, 30 minutes?

____

6. How many days are there in 4 weeks, 3 days?

____

7. Kendra watched two movies. The first lasted 100 minutes. The second lasted 1 hour, 55 minutes. Which movie was longer? By how many minutes?

____

____

____

8. **Writing to Explain** How many hours are there in a week? Explain how you found your answer.

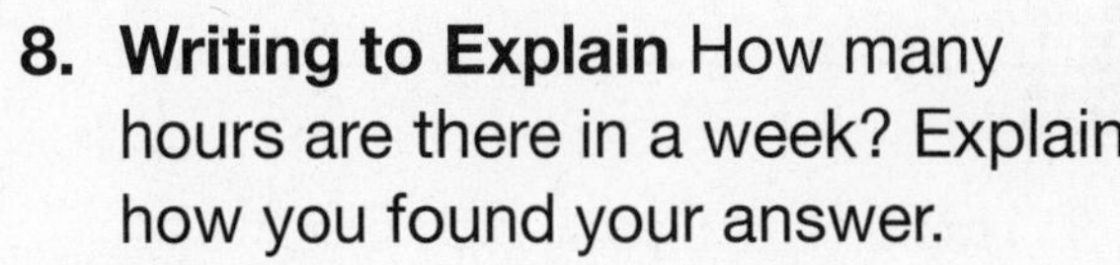

____

____

____

____

9. The Wilson family is going on a 5-week vacation through Australia and New Zealand this summer. How many days will the Wilson's be on vacation?

____

10. Lacy slept 8 hours last night. How many minutes did Lacy sleep?

A 400 **C** 640

B 480 **D** 800

Name ___________________________

Practice
17-4

Elapsed Time

Find the elapsed time.

1. Start Time: 6:00 P.M.
End Time: 7:15 P.M.

____

2. Start Time: 9:30 A.M.
End Time: 1:45 P.M.

____

3. Start Time: 3:10 P.M.
End Time: 4:00 P.M.

____

4. Start Time: 11:30 A.M.
End Time: 5:30 P.M.

____

5. Start Time: 7:30 A.M.
End Time: 10:50 A.M.

____

6. Start Time: 9:00 P.M.
End Time: 4:30 A.M.

____

7. Edie is a 1 year old. She naps from 12:45 P.M. to 2:30 P.M. each day. How long is Edie's nap?

____

8. Mr. Wellborn arrives at work at 8:40 A.M. He leaves for work 50 minutes before he arrives. At what times does Mr. Wellborn leave for work?

____

9. **Writing to Explain** How long is your school day? Explain how you found your answer.

____

____

____

____

10. Gary's father dropped him off at soccer practice at 2:45 P.M. His mother picked him up at 5:00 P.M. How long did soccer practice last?

A 2 hours 15 minutes

B 2 hours 25 minutes

C 3 hours 15 minutes

D 3 hours 25 minutes

Name ______________________

Temperature

Write each temperature in °F and °C.

1. 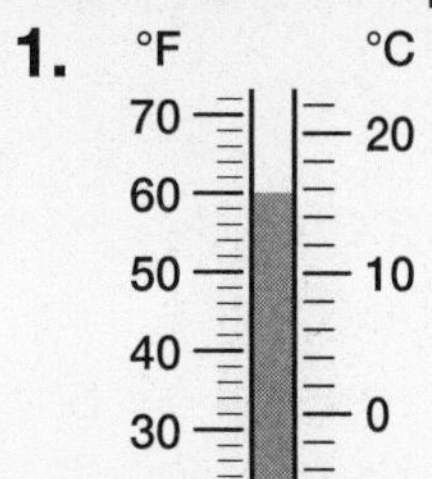

2. 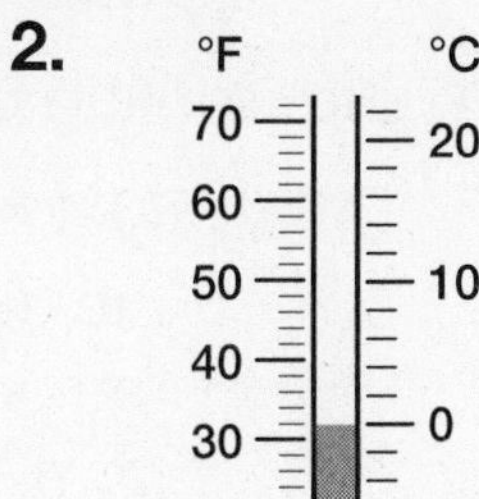

3. 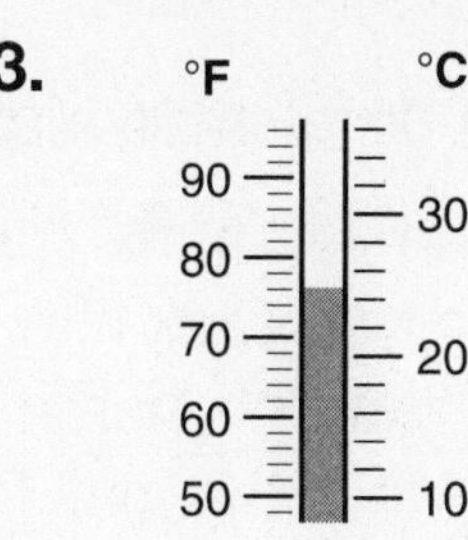

______________ ______________ ______________

______________ ______________ ______________

4. Reasonableness At 30°, Edgardo said the temperature was warm enough to go swimming. Did he mean to give the temperature in °F or °C? Explain.

____

____

____

5. The thermometer shows the high temperature in Helen's town Friday.

What was the high temperature in °F?

____

6. The normal high temperature in Dallas in January is 54°F. Which thermometer shows that temperature?

A 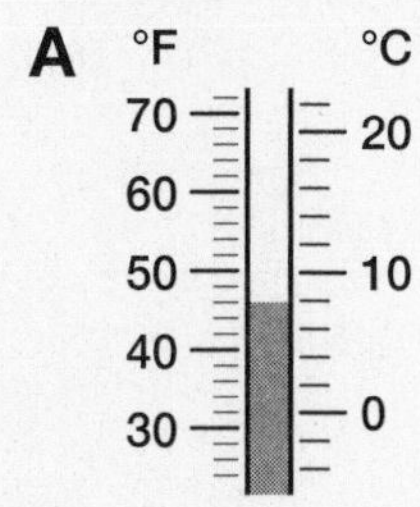

B 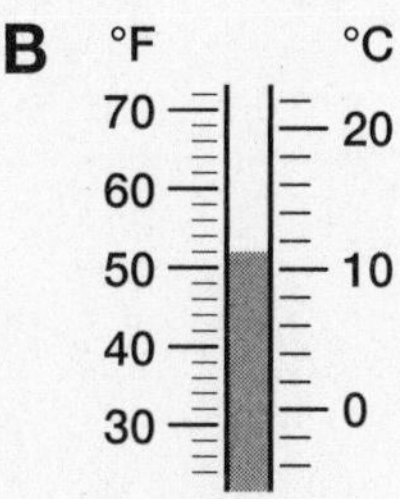

C 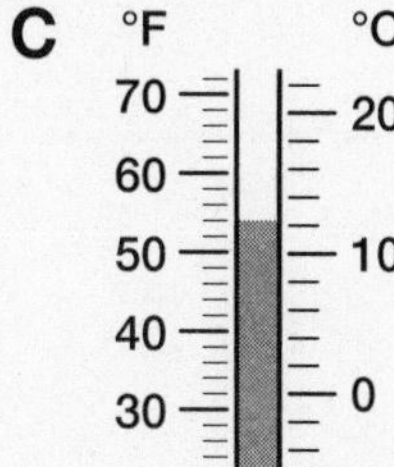

D 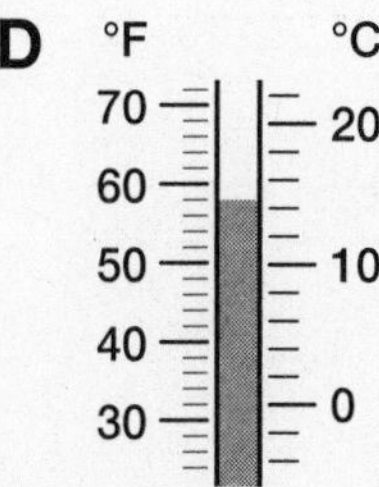

Name ______________________

Practice 17-6

Problem Solving: Work Backward

Solve the problem by drawing a picture and working backward.

1. Will arrived at his mother's office at 3 P.M. It took him 30 minutes to walk from his home to the mall. He was in the mall for 45 minutes. It then took him 15 minutes to walk to his mother's office. At what time did Will leave home?

____

2. At 12 noon, Leslie recorded the temperature as 56°F. The temperature had increased by 8°F from 10 A.M. The temperature at 8 A.M. was 2°F warmer than it was at 10 A.M. What was the temperature at 8 A.M.?

____

3. The test that Keyshawn's class took finished at 10:30 A.M. The first part of the test took 30 minutes. There was a 15-minute break. The second part of the test also took 30 minutes. At what time did the test start?

____

4. The temperature was 16°C when Becky returned home at 6 P.M. The temperature was 4°C warmer at 3 P.M. than it was at 6 P.M. It was 3°C warmer at 12 noon than it was at 3 P.M. What was the temperature at 12 noon?

____

5. Elliot finished studying at 4:45 P.M. He spent 30 minutes reading a social studies chapter. He spent 45 minutes on his math homework. In between reading and math, Elliot took a 20-minute break. At what time did Elliot begin studying?

   A 3:00 P.M. **B** 3:10 P.M. **C** 3:30 P.M. **D** 6:20 P.M.

Name ______________________

Practice **18-1**

Using Mental Math to Multiply

Find each product.

1. 3 × 10 ______

2. 6 × 100 ______

3. 9 × 1,000 ______

4. 80 × 3 ______

5. 4 × 700 ______

6. 2,000 × 5 ______

7. 6 × 400 ______

8. 800 × 8 ______

9. 6 × 900 ______

10. 90 × 7 ______

11. 3,000 × 4 ______

12. 500 × 4 ______

13. Ms. Armstrong works 40 hours each week. How many hours does she work in 4 weeks?

______

14. There are 2,000 pounds in one ton. How many pounds are there in 6 tons?

______

15. **Number Sense** A century is 100 years. How many years are there in 8 centuries?

______

16. One metric ton equals 1,000 kilograms. How many kilograms are there in 7 metric tons?

______

17. **Explain It** How can you use mental math to multiply 800 × 5?

____

____

____

18. Each time you pass "Start" on a board game you receive 300 points. How many points will you receive if you pass "Start" 6 times?

A 180 **B** 1,800 **C** 18,000 **D** 180,000

Name ____________________

Estimating Products

Estimate each product.

1. 5 × 53	**2.** 7 × 48	**3.** 6 × 58	**4.** 8 × 22	**5.** 3 × 73
6. 9 × 42	**7.** 4 × 93	**8.** 8 × 57	**9.** 6 × 52	**10.** 7 × 63
11. 8 × 54	**12.** 2 × 97	**13.** 6 × 78	**14.** 5 × 37	**15.** 7 × 58

16. Reasoning Marcia said that if she estimates 73 × 7, the product will be less than the exact answer. Is she correct? Explain.

17. Audrey delivers 38 newspapers each day of the week except Sunday. About how many newspapers does she deliver in a week? ________

18. Explain It Each video game at an arcade requires 55 tokens. Tom has 100 tokens. He said he can play 2 games. Is he correct? Explain.

19. A basketball player scores an average of 32 points per game. About how many points will he score in 8 games? ________

20. Which is the best estimate for 67 × 9?

A 540 **B** 630 **C** 670 **D** 700

Name ______________________

Practice
18-3

Multiplication and Arrays

Find each product. You may use place-value blocks or draw a picture to help.

1. 3 × 17

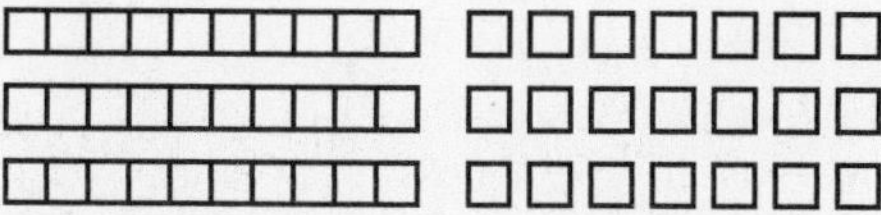

______

2. 2 × 22

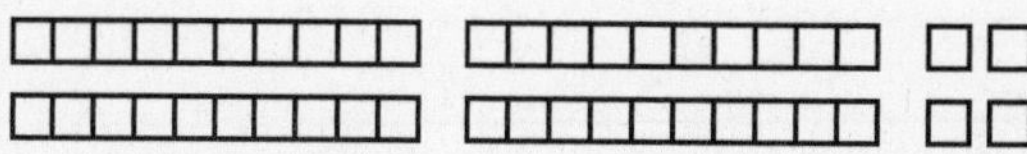

______

3. 5 × 34 ______

4. 4 × 13 ______

5. 3 × 57 ______

6. 2 × 34 ______

7. 6 × 22 ______

8. 3 × 43 ______

9. 5 × 26 ______

10. 6 × 18 ______

11. 4 × 24 ______

12. 5 × 29 ______

For **13** through **15**, use the table at the right.

Days Worked in April

Employee	Days Worked
Bob	19
Josh	25
Marvin	13

13. Bob works 7 hours each day. How many hours did he work in April all together?

______

14. Josh works 8 hours each day. How many hours did he work in April all together?

______

15. Marvin works 9 hours each day. How many more hours did Bob work than Marvin in April?

______

16. **Explain It** How can you use an array to find 4 × 13?

____

____

17. What is the product of 27 × 4?

A 36 **B** 88 **C** 108 **D** 127

Name ______________________

Practice
18-4

Breaking Apart to Multiply

Find each product. You may use place-value blocks or draw a picture to help.

1. 4 × 43 ______ **2.** 7 × 18 ______ **3.** 5 × 13 ______ **4.** 2 × 88 ______ **5.** 4 × 34 ______

6. 3 × 49 ______ **7.** 6 × 42 ______ **8.** 4 × 56 ______ **9.** 3 × 25 ______ **10.** 5 × 24 ______

11. 2 × 54 ______ **12.** 4 × 37 ______ **13.** 7 × 22 ______ **14.** 6 × 16 ______ **15.** 6 × 37 ______

16. A carpenter makes chairs with slats that run across the back of the chairs as shown. Each chair uses 7 slats. He needs to make 24 chairs. How many slats must he make?

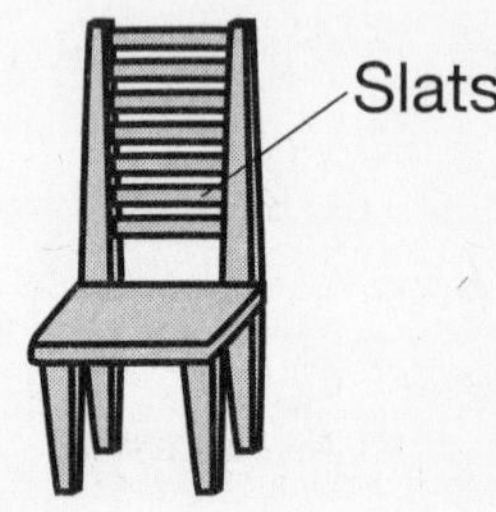

____

17. Each piece of wood trim is 6 feet long. Exactly 19 pieces are needed to go around a room. How many feet of wood trim are needed?

____

18. **Writing to Explain** How can you multiply 42 × 8 by breaking apart numbers?

____

19. A runner runs 34 miles each week. How many miles does the runner run in 5 weeks?

____

20. Which is equal to 5 × 25?

A 25 + 10 **B** 100 + 5 **C** 115 **D** 100 + 25

Name ______________________

Practice **18-5**

Using an Expanded Algorithm

In **1** and **2**, complete. In **3** through **5**, find each product. You may use place-value blocks or drawings to help.

1. $\begin{array}{r} 27 \\ \times\ 3 \\ \hline 21 \\ +\ \square\square \\ \hline \square\square \end{array}$

2. $\begin{array}{r} 43 \\ \times\ 5 \\ \hline 15 \\ +\ \square\square\square \\ \hline \square\square\square \end{array}$

3. $\begin{array}{r} 19 \\ \times\ 4 \\ \hline \end{array}$

4. $\begin{array}{r} 36 \\ \times\ 5 \\ \hline \end{array}$

5. 6 × 45 ______

Find each product. You may use place-value blocks or drawings to help.

6. $\begin{array}{r} 96 \\ \times\ 3 \\ \hline \end{array}$

7. $\begin{array}{r} 27 \\ \times\ 5 \\ \hline \end{array}$

8. $\begin{array}{r} 57 \\ \times\ 4 \\ \hline \end{array}$

9. $\begin{array}{r} 44 \\ \times\ 3 \\ \hline \end{array}$

10. 6 × 27 ______

11. An area in Norway gets sunlight all day for 14 weeks straight during the summer. How many days is 14 weeks?

______

12. There are 19 tables end-to-end in a line at a flea market. Each table is 6 feet long. How many feet long is the line of tables?

______

13. **Reasoning** Suppose you know that 9 × 20 = 180. How can you use this fact to find 9 × 24? Explain your strategy.

____

____

____

____

14. A pound is equal to 16 ounces. How many ounces are there in 6 pounds?

A 66 **B** 86 **C** 96 **D** 106

Name ______________________

Practice 18-6

Multiplying 2- and 3-Digit by 1-Digit Numbers

Estimate and then find each product. You may use drawings to help.

1. 48×4 **2.** 52×7 **3.** 36×3 **4.** 67×5 **5.** 4×33 ______

Find each product.

6. 53×4 **7.** 61×3 **8.** 74×4 **9.** 96×2 **10.** 5×57 ______

11. 3×487 ______ **12.** 632×4 ______ **13.** 8×275 ______ **14.** 396×5 ______

15. Bruce reads 35 pages of a book each day. It will take him 9 days to finish the book. How many pages are in the book?

______

16. **Estimation** Jose drinks 64 ounces of water each day. About how many fluid ounces of water does he drink each week?

______

17. **Reasonableness** Celeste multiplied $44 \times 5 = 202$. Is her product reasonable? Explain why or why not?

______

______

______

______

18. Each bus in the Turtle System can seat 48 passengers. How many passengers can be seated on 6 Turtle System buses?

A 248 **B** 252 **C** 268 **D** 288

Name ______________________

Practice 18-7

Problem Solving: Draw a Picture and Write a Number Sentence

1. At dress rehearsal Wednesday, there were 66 people in the audience. On opening night Thursday, there were 3 times as many people. How many people were in the audience for opening night?

Dress Rehearsal	66			
Opening Night	66	66	66	3 times as many

_______ people in all

2. At Heather and Bob's wedding, there were 32 tables. Each table seats 8 people. All of the tables were full. How many people attended the wedding?

_______ people in all

32	32	32	32	32	32	32	32

The chart shows the number of calories in fats, proteins, and carbohydrates. Use the chart for **3** through **5**.

3. The energy bar that Kyle is eating has 37 grams of carbohydrates. How many calories are from carbohydrates in the energy bar?

_______ calories in all

37	37	37	37

Nutritional Information

Ingredients	Calories Per Gram
Protein	4
Carbohydrate	4
Fat	9

4. A serving of chicken has 27 grams of protein and 3 grams of fat. How many calories are in a serving of chicken?

____

5. A banana has 27 grams of carbohydrates. It has a total of 121 calories. How many of its calories come from sources other than carbohydrates?

____

6. **Write a Problem** Write a problem that can be solved by drawing a picture. Draw the picture and solve the problem.

Name ____________________

Practice **19-1**

Mental Math

Use patterns to find each quotient.

1. 24 ÷ 4 ______

240 ÷ 4 ______

2,400 ÷ 4 ______

2. 42 ÷ 6 ______

420 ÷ 6 ______

4,200 ÷ 6 ______

3. 12 ÷ 3 ______

120 ÷ 3 ______

1,200 ÷ 3 ______

4. 25 ÷ 5 ______

250 ÷ 5 ______

2,500 ÷ 5 ______

5. 63 ÷ 7 ______

630 ÷ 7 ______

6,300 ÷ 7 ______

6. 64 ÷ 8 ______

640 ÷ 8 ______

6,400 ÷ 8 ______

Use mental math to find each quotient.

7. 240 ÷ 3 ______

8. 5,600 ÷ 8 ______

9. 1,000 ÷ 5 ______

10. 490 ÷ 7 ______

11. 1,500 ÷ 3 ______

12. A race is 1,600 yards long. The runners have to run 4 laps around the track. How many yards is each lap?

______

13. There were 80 people at a banquet. They were seated at 4 tables. Each table had the same number of people. How many people were at each table?

______

14. Writing to Explain How can you use a pattern to find 2,100 ÷ 3? What is the quotient?

______

______

15. On a cross-country trip, the Smiths drove 2,700 miles in 9 days. They drove the same number of miles each day. How many miles did they drive each day?

A 3 **C** 300

B 30 **D** 3,000

16. Number Sense How many $5 bills are there in $2,000?

______

Name ______________________

Practice 19-2

Estimating Quotients

Estimate each quotient.

1. 78 ÷ 8 ______
2. 221 ÷ 3 ______
3. 620 ÷ 9 ______
4. 225 ÷ 6 ______
5. 5,341 ÷ 8 ______
6. 537 ÷ 6 ______
7. 2,512 ÷ 4 ______
8. 348 ÷ 7 ______
9. 427 ÷ 7 ______
10. 1,925 ÷ 6 ______
11. 812 ÷ 9 ______
12. 1,253 ÷ 4 ______
13. 3,173 ÷ 8 ______
14. 2,833 ÷ 6 ______
15. 4,173 ÷ 5 ______

16. There are 365 days in a year. Elroy has piano practice once every 5 days. About how many times does Elroy have piano practice in a year?

______

17. A restaurant offers a buffet dinner for $9. The restaurant earned $5,517 in buffet dinner receipts last week. About how many dinners were served?

______

18. **Number Sense** Will the estimate of 537 ÷ 8 be less than or greater than the actual quotient? Explain your answer.

______

______

______

19. There are 225 students that signed up to play in a basketball league. Each team will have 8 players. About how many teams will there be?

A 2

B 20

C 3

D 30

Name ______________________

Practice
19-3

Connecting Models and Symbols

Use pictures or place-value blocks to help you find each quotient.

1. 42 ÷ 3 →

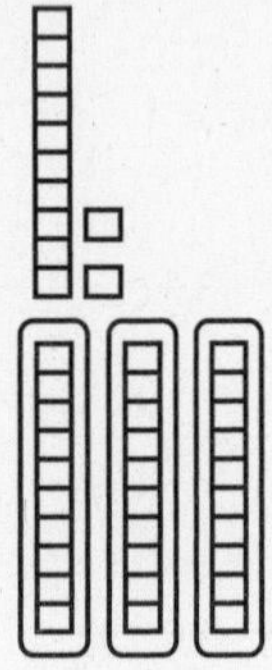

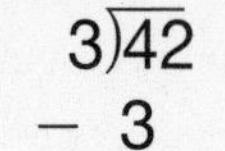

$3\overline{)42}$ → $3\overline{)42}$ − 3 → $3\overline{)42}$ − 3 − 0

Use pictures to help you find each quotient.

2. 54 ÷ 3 ______ **3.** 76 ÷ 2 ______ **4.** 95 ÷ 5 ______ **5.** 68 ÷ 4 ______ **6.** 90 ÷ 6 ______

7. 52 ÷ 2 ______ **8.** 78 ÷ 6 ______ **9.** 98 ÷ 7 ______ **10.** 48 ÷ 3 ______ **11.** 38 ÷ 2 ______

12. Trisha collected 4 times as many bugs as Shirley. Trisha collected 60 bugs. How many did Shirley collect?

______

13. Max bought 6 CDs for $96. All of the CDs cost the same amount. How much money did each CD cost?

______

14. Estimation Will the quotient of 63 ÷ 3 be greater than or less than 20? Explain.

______

______

______

15. Mrs. Wong baked 72 cookies on 4 cookie sheets. Each cookie sheet had the same number of cookies. How many cookies were on each cookie sheet?

A 14

B 16

C 17

D 18

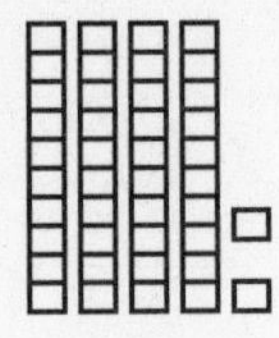

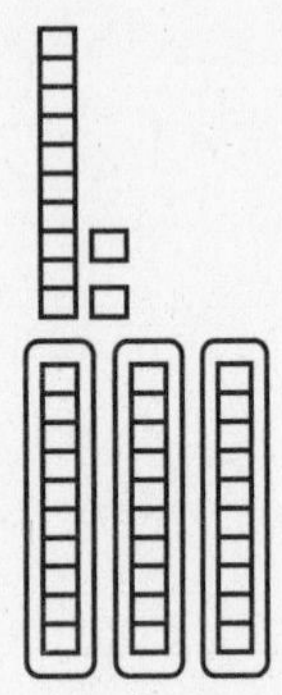

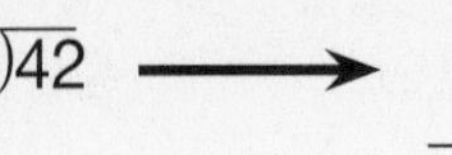

Name ______________________

Practice
19-4

Dividing 2-Digit Numbers

Complete. Find each quotient. Check your answers.

1. $3\overline{)96}$ quotient: 3 _; − 9; 6; − _; 0

2. $5\overline{)75}$ − _; _5; − _; _

3. $4\overline{)68}$ quotient: 1 _; − 40; _8; − _; 0

4. $2\overline{)98}$ − _; _8; − _; _

5. $6\overline{)78}$ − 6; _8; − _; 0

6. $3\overline{)69}$ − _; 9; − _; _

7. $5\overline{)65}$ quotient: 1 _; − _; _5; − _; 0

8. $4\overline{)56}$ − _; _6; − _; _

9. Jennifer has 57 fish. She wants to put them in 3 fish tanks. If she puts the same number of fish in each tank, how many fish will be in each tank?

____

10. There are 84 chairs in a restaurant. Each table in the restaurant has 6 chairs around it. How many tables does the restaurant have?

____

11. **Estimation** How can you use estimation to find the quotient of 57 ÷ 3?

____

____

____

____

12. Which has the greatest quotient?

A 75 ÷ 3

B 76 ÷ 4

C 72 ÷ 2

D 75 ÷ 5

Name ______________________

Dividing with Remainders

Complete. Check your answers.

1. $5\overline{)36}$
2. $7\overline{)36}$
3. $8\overline{)52}$

Find each quotient. Check your answers.

4. $6\overline{)45}$
5. $8\overline{)37}$
6. $3\overline{)20}$
7. $9\overline{)80}$
8. $7\overline{)38}$
9. $5\overline{)42}$
10. $7\overline{)62}$
11. $8\overline{)20}$

12. **Number Sense** Regina is going to divide a number by 8. What is the greatest remainder that she can have?

______

13. There are 43 girls signed up for cheerleading. Each cheerleading squad will have exactly 8 girls. How many squads will there be? How many girls will not be on a cheerleading squad?

______

14. **Reasoning** Each costume that Ms. Wren makes uses 3 yards of yarn. She has 26 yards of yarn. How many complete costumes can Ms. Wren make?

______

15. The chorus has 21 students. For a concert, they are being driven in cars that can each hold 4 students. How many cars are needed?

A 4
B 5
C 6
D 7

Name ______________________________

Practice
19-6

Problem Solving: Multiple-Step Problems

Solve. Answer the hidden question first.

1. Marcus counted a total of 40 wheels from bicycles and tricycles while sitting on a park bench. Marcus counted 11 bicycles. How many tricycles did Marcus count?

   ____

   HINT: Hidden Question—How many wheels did the bicycles have?

2. Julie bought 15 baseballs and some softballs. The total cost of the balls is $90. Each ball costs $5. How many softballs did Julie buy?

   ____

   HINT: How much money did Julie spend on baseballs?

3. Bert bought 4 books for $7 each and a magazine for $5. He paid with a $50 bill. How much money did Bert receive back from the cashier?

   ____

   HINT: Hidden Question—How much money did Bert spend?

4. A community group bought 12 student tickets and 3 adult tickets to the movies. The total cost of the tickets was $96. Student tickets cost $6. How much money does an adult ticket cost?

   ____

   HINT: How much money did the group spend on student tickets?

5. There are 48 students in the band. The boys and girls are in separate rows. There are 6 students in each row. There are 3 rows of boys. How many rows of girls are there?

   ____

   HINT: Hidden Question—How many boys are there?

6. **Write a Problem** Write a real-world problem that can be solved by finding and answering a hidden question.

   ____

   ____

   ____

Name ______________________

Organizing Data

For **1** through **6**, use the survey data at the right.

1. Make a tally chart for the data.

Favorite Type of Music		
Rock	Jazz	Country
Jazz	Rock	Rock
Rock	Country	Rap
Country	Rock	Rap
Country	Country	Country
Rap	Rap	Rock
Country	Rap	Jazz
Rap	Jazz	Country
Country	Rock	Rap

2. How many people were surveyed in all?

____

3. Which type of music was picked by the most people?

____

4. Which type of music was picked by the fewest people?

____

5. Which two types of music were picked by the same number of people?

____

6. **Writing to Explain** How does making a tally chart help you to organize data?

____

____

____

7. **Number Sense** Which number is represented by 卌 卌 卌 ||||?

A 16

B 17

C 19

D 20

Name ____________________

Reading Pictographs and Bar Graphs

For **1** through **4**, use the pictograph at the right.

1. Who read the most books?

____

2. Who read exactly 18 books?

____

3. How many more books did Nancy read than Jamal?

____

4. Who read the fewest books?

____

For **5** through **8**, use the bar graph at the right.

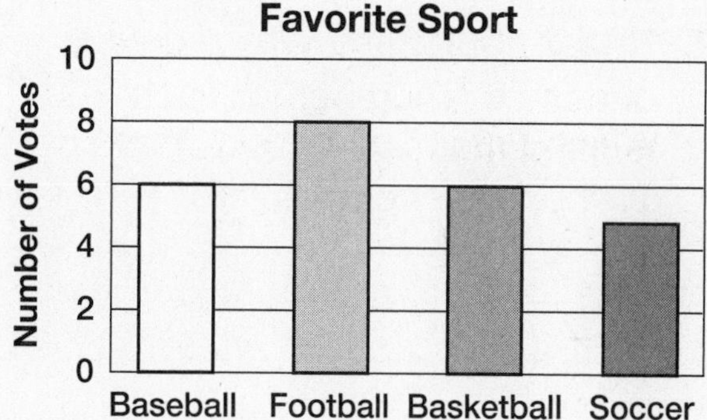

5. How many people chose soccer as their favorite sport?

____

6. Which sport was chosen as the favorite?

____

7. **Reasonableness** Casey said that 40 people were surveyed. Is his answer reasonable? Explain.

____

____

____

8. Which sentence is true?

A Baseball and basketball received the same number of votes.

B More people chose soccer than baseball.

C More people chose football than basketball and soccer combined.

D More people chose baseball than football.

Name ___________________________________

Practice
20-3

Making Pictographs

For **1** and **2**, use the chart.

1. Make a pictograph to show the data in the chart. Write a title. Choose the key.

Color of Cars

Color	Tally	Number
Red	~~IIII~~ ~~IIII~~ ~~IIII~~ I	16
Green	~~IIII~~ ~~IIII~~ ~~IIII~~ ~~IIII~~	20
Silver	~~IIII~~ ~~IIII~~ ~~IIII~~ ~~IIII~~ IIII	24
Black	~~IIII~~ ~~IIII~~ IIII	14

2. Reasonableness Why did you choose the number for each symbol that you chose?

____

____

____

3. Fred is going to make a pictograph showing the number of tomatoes that he picked each day. He picked 30 Monday, 25 Tuesday, 35 Wednesday, and 40 Thursday. Which would be the best number to use for each symbol?

A 1
B 2
C 5
D 20

4. Explain It Pamela made a pictograph showing students' favorite drinks. Pamela drew 3 glasses to represent the 6 students who chose chocolate milk. Is her pictograph correct? Explain.

Favorite Drinks

Drink	Number of Students
Chocolate milk	🥛🥛🥛
Fruit juice	🥛🥛🥛🥛

Key Each 🥛 = 2 students.

____

____

____

Name ______________________________

Making Bar Graphs

For **1** and **2**, use the chart at the right.

Favorite States to Visit

State	Number of Votes
New York	25
Florida	35
California	30
Hawaii	20

1. Make a bar graph to show the data in the chart.

2. Reasoning How can you use a bar graph to determine which state had the least number of votes?

____

____

3. Explain It Describe your process for determining the scale for a bar graph.

____

____

____

4. The table at the right shows the number of phone calls Mrs. Walker made during 5 days of fundraising. Which is the scale you would use to make a bar graph of the data?

Fundraising Calls

Day	Phone Calls
Saturday	26
Sunday	19
Monday	20
Tuesday	24
Wednesday	16

A by 1s
B by 2s
C by 5s
D by 10s

Name ____________________

Ordered Pairs and Line Graphs

Write the ordered pair for each point on the grid.

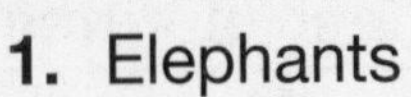

1. Elephants ________ **2.** Train Station ________

3. Hippos ________ **4.** Snakes ________

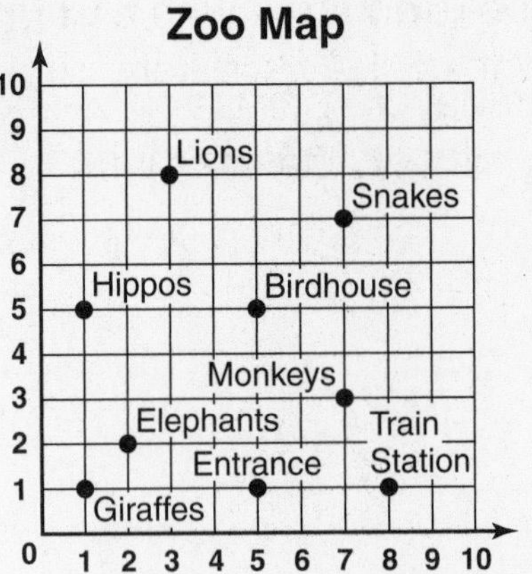

Identify the location named by each ordered pair.

5. (7, 3) ________ **6.** (5, 5) ________ **7.** (5, 1) ________ **8.** (3, 8) ________

For **9** through **12**, use the line graph.

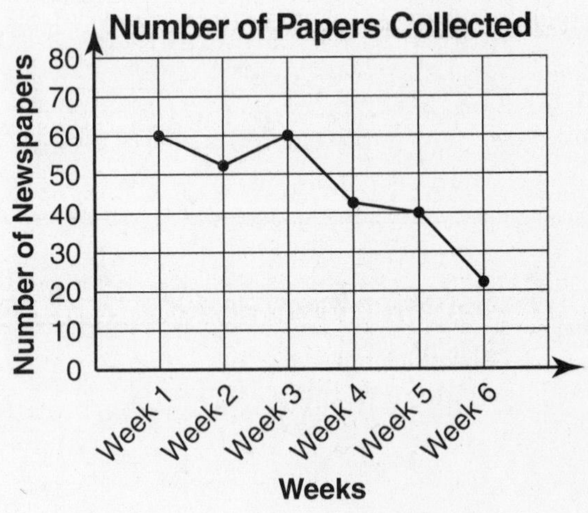

9. How many newspapers were collected in Week 1? ________

10. How many more newspapers were collected in Week 3 than Week 5?

____

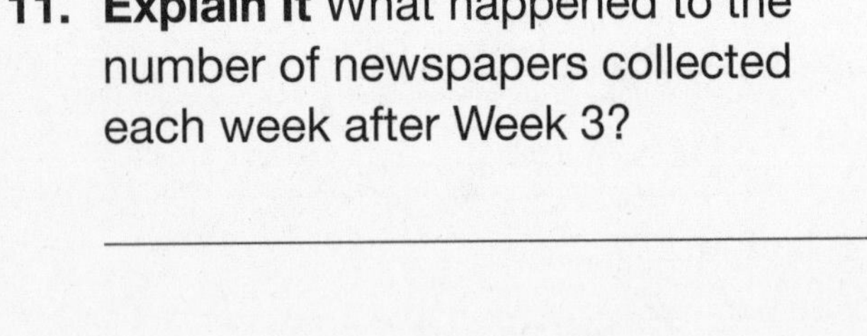

11. Explain It What happened to the number of newspapers collected each week after Week 3?

____

____

____

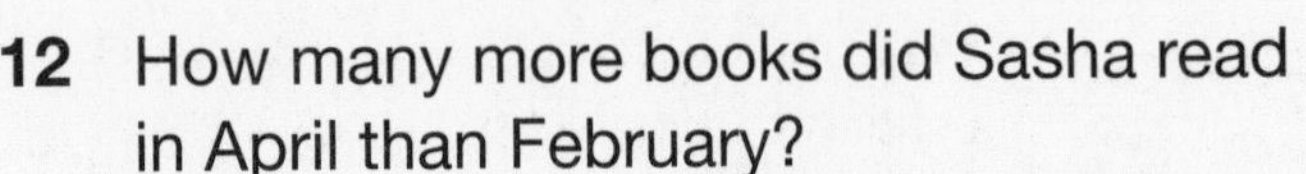

12 How many more books did Sasha read in April than February?

A 2 **C** 5

B 4 **D** 7

Name ___________________________

Practice
20-6

How Likely?

Gene is an adult with a dog named Bob. Describe each event as likely, unlikely, impossible, or certain.

1. Bob will sleep tonight.

____

2. Bob will weigh more than Gene.

____

3. Bob will eat.

____

4. Bob will read a book.

____

For **5** through **8,** use the spinner at the right.

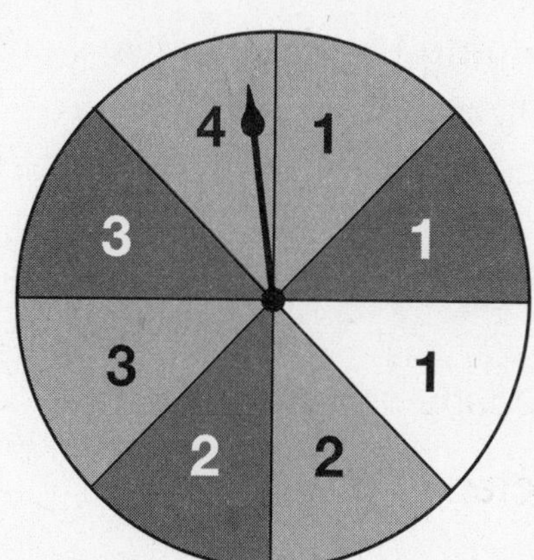

5. What outcome is more likely than 2?

____

6. What outcomes are equally likely?

____

7. Describe the chance of the spinner landing on 5.

____

8. What outcome is less likely than a 3?

____

9. Explain It What is the difference between a likely event and an unlikely event?

____

____

____

____

10. Dana and Rose are playing a card game. Dana has cards with 3 circles, 4 squares, 2 triangles, and 1 rectangle. If Rose picks one card from Dana's hand without looking, which card will she most likely pick?

A circle **B** square **C** triangle **D** rectangle

Name ______________________________

Outcomes and Experiments

For **1** through **3**, use the spinner to the right and the table below.

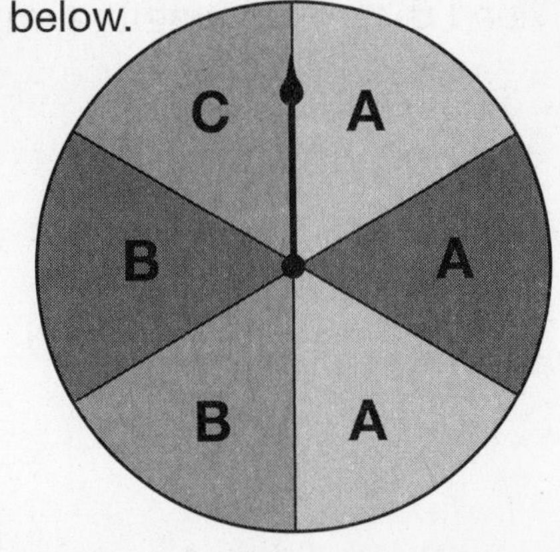

1. Complete the table.

A	3	6		12	15		45
B	2	4	6	8		20	30
C	1	2	3	4	5	10	
Total Spins	6	12	18		30	60	

2. Reasoning Predict what is likely to happen in 120 spins.

____

____

____

3. Do the experiment using a number cube. Let 1, 2, and 3 represent A; 4 and 5 represent B; and 6 represent C. Toss the number cube 30 times. See if it matches your prediction above. What happened?

____

____

____

4. In a probability experiment, the spinner results were 10 blue, 10 red, and 30 green. Which spinner most likely gave these results?

A

blue red green

B

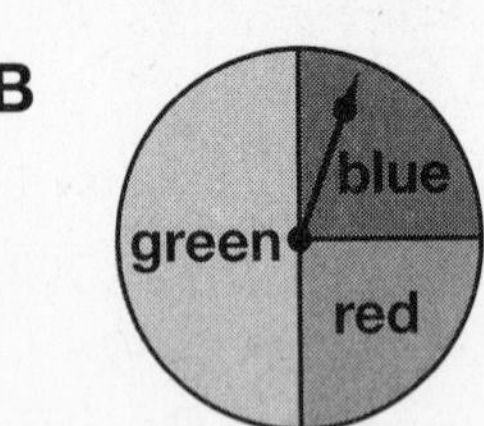

C

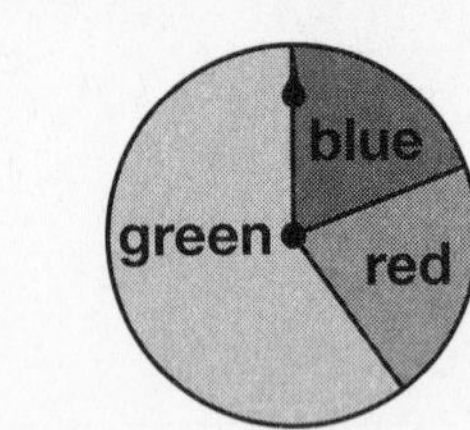

D

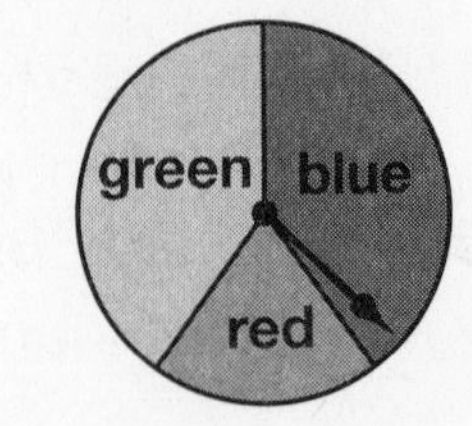

Name ______________________________

Line Plots and Probability

For **1** through **5**, use the data at the right.

1. Make a line plot to show the data.

Number of Points Katie Scored

Game	Pts	Game	Pts	Game	Pts
1	23	11	25	21	24
2	25	12	30	22	26
3	30	13	27	23	25
4	25	14	22	24	28
5	21	15	26	25	27
6	26	16	21	26	26
7	21	17	29	27	29
8	24	18	25	28	30
9	28	19	21	29	22
10	20	20	23	30	24

2. How many Xs do you show for 24 points?

____

3. Which number of points did Katie only score once?

____

4. Which number of points did Katie score the most?

____

5. Which two point totals did Katie score exactly four times each?

____

For **6** and **7**, use the line plot at the right.

6. How many fewer students read 5 books than 8 books?

____

7. How many students read less than 7 books?

A 11 **C** 17

B 14 **D** 22

Books Read in May

3 4 5 6 7 8 9 10

Number of Books Read

Name ______________________________

Practice
20-9

Problem Solving: Use Tables and Graphs to Draw Conclusions

Use the pictographs for **1** through **4**.

Girls Shoes Sold at Just Shoes

Sneakers	
Sandals	
Pumps	
Boots	

Girls Shoes Sold at All Shoes

Sneakers	
Sandals	
Pumps	
Boots	

Each = 10 shoes. Each = 5 shoes.

1. Which type of shoe was sold the most at Just Shoes?

____

2. Which two types of shoes were sold equally at All Shoes?

____

3. Which store sold the most pumps?

____

4. How many sneakers were sold in all?

____

For **5** and **6**, use the bar graph at the right.

5. How many cars were washed altogether?

____

6. **Write a Problem** Write a word problem different from Exercise 5 that can be solved by reading the graph.

____

____

Cars Washed by Grade

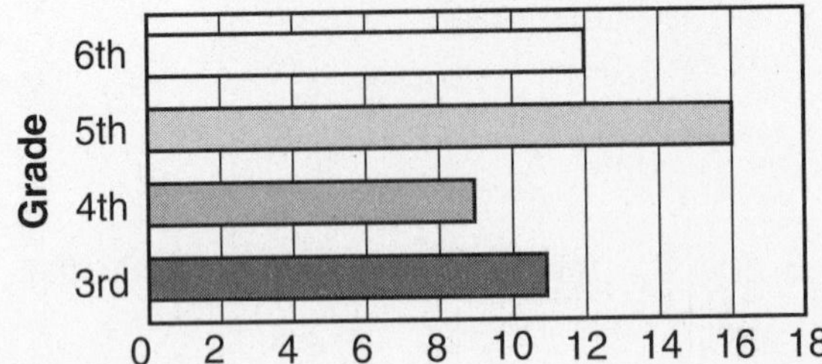

7. According to the tally chart, how many more students received an A or a B in Test 2 than in Test 4?

____

Students Receiving an A or a B

Test	Tally
1	𝍸 𝍸 ||
2	𝍸 𝍸 𝍸 |
3	𝍸 𝍸 𝍸
4	𝍸 |||